Alone To Think

Thoughts About Our Failing Correctional And Criminal Systems And How To Fix Them

by

Alan L. Watts, M.D.

authorHOUSE™

1663 LIBERTY DRIVE, SUITE 200
BLOOMINGTON, INDIANA 47403
(800) 839-8640
WWW.AUTHORHOUSE.COM

First published by AuthorHouse 09/19/05

ISBN: 1-4208-7001-7 (e)
ISBN: 1-4208-7000-9 (sc)

Printed in the United States of America
Bloomington, Indiana

This book is printed on acid-free paper.

This Book is Dedicated to:

…all those souls who were not rehabilitated in our current correctional system…

…the hard-working correctional workers whose experience and understanding are thwarted by our liberal, activist, judiciary system…

…reclaiming our streets and communities from the thugs and predators…

…placing the rights of citizens and victims above the rights we extend to the criminals…

…happier times before the welfare and entitlement programs fostered and supported a permanent underclass that produces a disproportionate amount of crime…

…those Americans, who, through hard work and dedication maintain the moral fiber that has made this country great.…

Acknowledgments

I would like to thank Charlene Kovach for her many hours of typing, revising, word processing, and editing. For her many hours at the computer, in the library, and on the telephone. For her tireless efforts to complete this book and make Iso-Rehab a reality. I could not have done it without her.

I offer my thanks to each of the dedicated authors listed in the bibliography who have devoted countless hours, years, and careers researching the penal and correctional systems and the causes of the breakdown in American society that has led to the increase in violence and crime.

Contents

•Throughout this book the word "he" is used to refer to the criminal. American crime statistics indicate that the majority of criminals are of the masculine gender. He, as used herein, applies to both sexes and reads easier than the constant use of he/she. There is no sexist implication in the use of the word "he". Using the plural 'they' or 'their' is acceptable, but here again, "he" imparts more directness and clarity. 'He', 'she', 'they', and 'their' are used for clarity.

Preface

Kidnapping Victim Found Dead. Prime suspect violated parole. Police records reveal several sexual assaults and rapes. Possible connection of suspect to unsolved murder two years ago....

I read news items like this every day. I am growing weary of the crime and violence that surround my neighborhood. I am tired of always having to lock my car and house and even then wonder if I am safe. I am tired of being held hostage in my house, my city, and my country because of the criminal element that is allowed to walk the streets and threaten my very existence. Gone are the days of feeling safe in one's own home, yard, and neighborhood.

I am tired of society being blamed for the "root causes" of crime and being mandated to 'pay up' with tax dollars for assistance programs. These very programs have resulted in a multitude of problems that we are all drowning in today. I am tired of failing programs, such as welfare, which continue to consume more and more of my hard-earned tax dollars each year. Recipients take advantage of the temporary assistance and become dependent on it for their livelihood and milk it for all it is worth. I am fed up with supporting such programs.

I am tired of the disregard for responsible behavior and accountability for one's actions. The enemies include not only the criminals, but judges, the courts, and the prison system. I am tired of judges, lawyers, and a judicial system that stymies truth and justice and attempts to weaken or degrade the intent of our laws and our constitution. I am disgusted with plea bargaining for lesser charges that often returns criminals onto the streets. I am tired of the liberal mindset that champions prisoner rights over the rights of law-abiding citizens. I feel ashamed for our liberal judges who bend over backwards and loosely interpret the United States Constitution to further the agenda of political activists, ruthless lawyers, and inflate their own egos. I cringe when I hear criminals, by way of their lawyers demanding items that insure their comfort while they are in prison. Prisoners are suing because their rights have been violated and judges are giving into this foolish litigation. How much farther do we follow this insane path before we realize this is not what justice is all about? What is happening to the law-abiding, taxpayers' rights to security and protection from criminals? What is happening to the victims of criminal behavior?

I am frustrated with the criminals and their lawyers dictating the rules to the law-abiding citizens. I am tired of offenders not serving their full sentence and being released early because of overcrowding in prisons. I am fed up with paying millions of dollars to shelter, feed, clothe, and treat criminals in expensive, massive prisons with numerous amenities for pleasure, exercise, and education. Despite these "rehabilitative" methods, criminals usually continue their criminal activity once they return to the streets. Whatever happened to prisons being a place of punishment for criminal behavior? Where did America go wrong?

I recall my undergraduate days in college studying to become a sociologist with a minor in psychology. The classes in criminology were very slanted. They stressed ad nauseam that criminals were a product of their environment. I learned that criminals were practically forced into a life of crime by the forces of society. Criminologists were interested in treating these forces, which we now call "root causes," of crime.

One of the most perceived "root causes" of crime is poverty and discrimination. Criminologists, sociologists, psychologists, and the liberal left use poverty and discrimination as a crime producing milieu from which no one can escape. Tell this to the Jews, the Irish, and the Asians who were poor, lived in ghettos and slums, but worked hard and educated themselves out of poverty and their low-life environments.

Every possible rehabilitative scheme has been thought of and encouraged as a solution for criminal activity. The reduction in perceived punishment was accomplished by pushing for more prisoner freedom and increased prisoner benefits. Concern for society and the victims of crime was a nonissue in criminology. Nowhere was mention made of trying to teach criminals moral values and respect for the law. Emphasis on rehabilitation and treatment of criminals was the prime factor in the criminology agenda of the day.

I can reflect today on the false perceptions and programs that were developed by the faulty criminology of the time. Today, we all live in a much more violent America than we did in my undergraduate days. I must admit that much of the violence is a direct product of the failed penal policies that were adopted then, and are still being used today. Being disillusioned by the direction sociology and criminology were headed, I changed my major to medicine.

Working as a physician in a busy emergency room, I have experienced the effects of the "knife and gun club" —the direct victims of our urban violence. This first hand experience with our current level of violence is frightening. It is a tragic waste to see a teenager bleed out and die before your very eyes. The victim of a gang murder or a drive-by shooting. It happens almost on a daily basis in every large city in our country. It is all the more sobering when I realize that much of the mayhem is caused by known felons with long criminal records. Two and three time losers who are free to roam our city streets. Criminals turned loose by our courts and penal systems—free to prey upon unsuspecting citizens.

I am weary of these problems that plague our streets, courts, and prisons. This frustration has prompted me to create a different concept in the area of prison reform that is long overdue. I want to return to safe homes, streets, and neighborhoods in this country and so I offer this new approach to prisons in America.

Introduction

Everyday, almost continually, we hear and read reports of crime from our radios, televisions, and in our newspapers. A substantial percentage of these crime reports concern previously known felons and convicted criminals that are committing the crimes being reported. Our criminal-correctional system is not working. Our correctional system is, in fact, a multibillion dollar boondoggle that is helping to bankrupt American citizens. Any private corporation with the results similar to the American Criminal Correctional system would have gone out of business long ago — not so our correctional system.

Today we build overly expensive prisons, correctional facilities, and make sure that prisoners have proper medical care (better than they had before they were confined), recreational environments, good housing, and good nutrition. We allow prisoners to further their educations, write books, have visitors, use drugs within the prison system, and even control some of their gangs and criminal enterprises outside the prison walls. Prisoners can participate in sports and compete in sporting competitions. There is a move on to allow prisoners to have concerts and even sell their music (records) to the general public. They already have the ability to publish books they may have written while incarcerated.

We find that there is a definite pecking order within the prison walls. Prisoners that were convicted of the most brutal and heinous acts are generally at the top of the prisoner hierarchy.

We also see gangs that have taken over the prisons. Arrested and convicted gang members are often put in prisons where many of their old friends and gang buddies are serving time. They control other prisoners and the guard structure of the prison by controlling the prisoners and causing or preventing turmoil and prison riots.

There has recently been efforts by liberal citizens, or should I say progressive citizens, to allow "rap" type concerts to be broadcast from prisons, and to be aired on the national media. Some liberals don't think that prisoners should loose any of their citizen rights. Oh, well.

The need to publish *Alone to Think* is much more demanding today, 2005, than it was when I first wrote it back in 1994. At that time we had about 1.3 million people behind bars and in the correctional system. Today we have over 2.3 million people in our correctional system and crime is running rampant throughout America. We the people, need protection from criminals and the people that do not obey our laws.

We have a growing number of illegal immigrants entering our country on a daily basis. There is a growing percentage of illegal immigrants in our prisons, and the problem is getting worse. We were all immigrants when we migrated to this country; however, we came legally — we did not brake the law. Today, the politicians, the corporate employers, and anyone else who can make a buck or get a vote bends over backwards to help the law-breakers who enter this country illegally. It has become so bad that some of our politicians, such as Hillary Clinton, want to give felons, and ex-felons the right to vote in our electoral process.

Many of these gang members have a nicer life within the prison walls than they had on the outside before they were imprisoned. They have good food, a good place to sleep, good medical care, educational opportunities, and the ability to socialize with home buddies they knew on the outside. They have access to drugs, and can sexually abuse other inmates that are not their friends or not in their prison gangs. They learn how to become better criminal upon their release and not to be caught as easily the next time they commit a crime.

Historically, prisons have been viewed as places of punishment. Wrongdoers had to pay for their misbehavior and injury to other people and the crimes they committed. Since most criminals had no means or money to repay their victims, the offenders were sent to prison to atone for their crimes and to be punished. Public floggings, stocks and pillories, thumb screws and racks were used as punishment for offenders of the laws. These public displays had a deterrent effect for all citizens.

With the increased availability of untapped manpower collecting in prisons, punishment took on the form of work. The labor prescribed as "punishment" was not much different from what farm hands and many laborers performed on the outside on a daily basis. The prisoners were trained, were housed in secure buildings, ate better food than on the outside, and received medical care. Over the years, prisons became crowded, the work teams and chain gangs were increasingly difficult to control outside the prison walls. Repeat offenders were taking up significant prison space. With numerous prisoners behind bars, internal strife and friction between prisoners and the staff became perilous. Prisons began to provide recreational facilities and allow organized athletics to help maintain peace and harmony within the prison. The sting of punishment through incarceration was lessened.

What remained and what was interpreted as punishment was simple incarceration. The mere fact of separating a person from the home environment by incarceration in a prison was considered punishment. People began to protest that punishment and incarceration had no deterrent value since the rate of crime continued to rise. Punishment in the modern prison did not fit the pattern of punishment as most of us understood punishment.

Incarceration simply separates a person from family, friends, and familiar surroundings. Incarceration today does not really separate the "prisoner" from his previous environment. Many of today's prisoners join, and re-associate with their "home-boys" while in the prison context. Often, the incarceration substitutes a precarious form of survival with a stable environment with shelter and food. Incarceration, as a modified form of punishment, no longer has any sting. There is no punishment in our present penal systems. Even the death penalty, the most severe form of punishment, allows an average of eight to fifteen years of waiting on death row because of the court appeal process. Today, the death penalty is almost never carried out to completion. No wonder critics of penal institutions correctly state that punishment has no value in reducing the rate of crime and recidivism. Punishment, as practiced today, does not deter crime.

Simple incarceration has been compared to warehousing of prisoners solely to remove them from society. Warehousing alone has little, if any, deterrent effect on recidivism and the rate of criminal activity once the convict has served time and is released back into society. If the statistics on recidivism ever decreases it will probably be due to prisoners learning how to commit a crime and not get caught — a subject that is taught while in prison by associating and learning from professional criminals who have become their buddies.

The Quakers introduced the idea of the "reform school" into penal philosophy. Thus was born the thought to try to "rehabilitate" the criminals and hopefully decrease the amount of repeat offenders. With that, our prisons became "correctional facilities" and more of our tax dollars were devoted to rehabilitation programs. Increased staffing was necessary, along with programs for criminals whenever new and larger prisons were built.

With numerous years of rehabilitative programs to analyze, we have found that the rehabilitative efforts have failed. This is evident when one considers the high recidivism rates. Bureau of Justice Statistics from 1994 show an estimated 67% of persons released from prisons were rearrested within three years. Current media reports indicate released prisoners are continuing to commit crimes.

We find we are not rehabilitating criminals: we are merely housing them in expensive, comfortable quarters. Besides removal from family members, the only real punishment associated with modern prisons is the ever-present, unwelcome friction with other inmates. The top priority of many prisons today is maintaining peace and harmony between inmates, between prisoners and the staff, and between the prison and the community. What seems to remain is an aggressive effort to make prisoners more comfortable while in prison and a heightened awareness of prisoners' rights. We have truly gone astray from the original idea and theory of prisons as places of punishment for criminal activity.

Alone to Think explores the changes that have taken place over the years, and how the original intent of punishment and confinement have become blurred by liberal, activist judges, ruthless defense lawyers, and prisoner advocates who put the rights of the criminal above the rights of the law-abiding citizen. Current data illustrates how these changes have not improved the current correctional systems nor the criminals that return to the streets of our communities.

Alone to Think considers necessary steps needed to change our judicial system and make it responsive to the public interest. Aren't you tired of the mentality that says—commit a crime and you deserve a free education, job training, free medical coverage, food and housing, and government assistance to support your family while you receive prisoner rights and entitlements? The move is on today, if liberals have their way, to even grant prisoners the right to vote.

Americans are fed up with politicians throwing tax dollars at failed entitlement programs that actually breed and foster increasing crime rates. We hear the old excuse that we can't afford to lock up all the criminals. Really? With all the perks and frivolous spending that goes on in Congress, I should think that we could spend some money doing what taxpayers are demanding—lock up the criminals and get them off our streets! As criminals are being released early because of prison overcrowding, the lawmakers repeat the same old excuses—we don't have room for all the criminals. Well, let's tell the lawmakers to make room. If it takes warehousing of criminals to get them off the streets—so be it. We can build much cheaper facilities. I am in favor of doing whatever is necessary to restore peace and tranquillity to our homes, our communities, our country.

Alone to Think reviews current penal practices. Practices that have championed prisoner freedom and have failed to rehabilitate. Practices that have fostered an increase in repeat offenders and failed to reduce the rate of crime. Practices that make our correctional facilities unsafe for inmates who risk being assaulted, murdered, and raped at the hands of other inmates — and where the incidence of AIDS, HIV, and Hepatitis C is running rampant because of rape and sodomy. And, practices that have allowed our correctional institutions to be known as centers for advanced criminal studies.

A chapter will review the present price tag attached to our security and protection. It discusses the exorbitant cost of prison construction, prisoner confinement, and staffing. *Alone to Think* offers an alternative: a truly enlightened prison design and structure that is cost-effective, easy to build, expandable, and less expensive to staff and maintain. Most importantly, the design of this facility is safe for each inmate and provides an atmosphere conducive to learning and hopefully rehabilitating inmates.

The newest and most promising concept presented herein is the Isolation-Rehabilitation—Iso-Rehab—philosophy. This dual concept reveals a new method of prisoner control and protection along with an appropriate atmosphere to provide behavior modification, learning, and training. Isolation of prisoners is an important tool in prisoner control, safety and the rehabilitation process. Inmates are housed in single cell modules. where they eat, sleep, and exercise. The cell layout and design of the facility is an essential part of the Iso-Rehab philosophy and will be discussed. Floor plans are illustrated and specifications offered. Basic costs of design and materials are included. The benefits and complete format of this prison idea are detailed. The Iso-Rehab concept will insure the safety of criminals and law-abiding citizens and has a better chance at true rehabilitation of criminals.

Iso-Rehab was born out of concern for the rise in crime and the failings of the current prisons and their rehabilitation processes. I have tried not to bore you with pages of statistics that show how the U.S. is becoming the most crime-infested country on the face of the earth. The dismal crime figures can be obtained free through your states' correctional departments. Most newspapers publish crime statistics all too frequently as they report local, state, and national crimes. It is out of a growing concern for this nation that I offer the thoughts of this book.

I have presented some new ideas that could help our failing prison system. This Iso-Rehab prison concept addresses and answers overcrowding and other problems running rampant in today's prisons. It proposes safe and humane treatment of prisoners as well as protecting the staff. With this proposal we can afford to get the criminals off our streets and out of our communities, keep them locked up safely for the entire length of their sentence, and hopefully change their thought processes to eliminate, or at least reduce, the impulse to commit crime.

Many people may find the proposals controversial. Some may find the proposals strange and unusual. Let me assure you, the proposals are well thought out and sound. All proposals made herein can be defended strongly by showing the failure and irrational thinking that is the basis of our current system. I hope when you read this book, you will do so with an open mind. I hope that you can realize the sincerity and concern these concepts have for true rehabilitation of our lost souls—the citizens that have erred and gone wrong—the criminals. Consider these proposals with the realization that there is a need for change. It truly can be the answer to today's problems with criminals and prisons.

I originally wrote this book with the thought of publishing it in 1994. I went through the steps of registration and copy-writing, but did not follow through with publishing. However, since 1994, and especially in 2004 and 2005 this country is plagued with a rising crime rate and an increase in crime by repeat offenders who have been released from "correctional" facilities.

Please bear with me if some of the crime statistics listed seem out of date — they were obtained using 1990s information. Those statistics, the crime rates, the "correctional" expenses, and the crimes committed by repeat offenders have all increased.

Because of the increasing crime rates, the increase in recidivism, the increase in sex crimes (especially against children), and the failure of our penal system, I felt I had to publish *Alone to Think* now!

Chapter One

An Overview of Crime

Can We Cure Crime?

The United States is becoming the most lawless country in the world. The daily mass media and television news reports depict the violence that walks unabated throughout our land especially in our urban centers. Our newspapers report senseless murders, rapes, robberies, and gang shootings on a daily basis. Cries for gun control, stiffer sentences, longer incarceration, and a tougher stance against crime are heard throughout the country. Amidst all this chaos and fright we look down our noses at other countries and call them police states because of their efforts to control their criminals. We know we have a serious problem with crime and violence here in the U.S.A., but we seem to be unable to control it.

Most Americans are tired of what's happening to our country and to our level of fear. People are worried about their safety and security. We live trapped in our houses with barricaded doors, bars on our windows, and every conceivable lock and safety device. In communities in the United States, people live in fear, people are held hostage in their own homes, people are mortally afraid of leaving their doors unlocked. My own mother, who is 86 years old and lives alone in her own home, barricades herself behind locked doors as the sun sets. This is a sad commentary for "the land of the free and the home of the brave". The ever-increasing incidence of violent crimes in the country demands that the government take steps to control the violence and protect the people by enforcing the laws.

One of the primary responsibilities of government is to protect its citizenry. It accomplishes this through the creation of laws. Laws that should reflect the mores and standards of the society. The essence of law is force. Laws are hollow and meaningless without the power of enforcement. With force, laws become tools to help insure the smooth and efficient management of a lawful society. The American people created the laws and are therefore obligated to obey the laws. When laws are broken society has two possible courses of action. First, use the force necessary to insure compliance with the law. Second, reevaluate the law to see if the law fits the needs of the society.

We have enormous police forces and we pay a dear price for the protection we receive because of their presence. We have more policemen per capita and more policemen visible than most other countries. In addition to the great number of our municipal and state police units, we also have over a million private security policemen. One would think that with so many policemen in the U.S. we would be safe and crime would be on the decline. Not so. We are hearing a cry for even more policemen and private security forces.

Why do we need so many policemen? Why aren't the present forces of policemen enforcing the laws? Our police corps are more of a reactive force than a deterrent force. They respond to a crime after the fact. Until recent court rulings; police officers would enforce the laws with the necessary force and apprehend criminal suspects. However, since the Rodney King beating, follow-up trials, and the Los Angeles riots, policemen have become more reluctant and hesitant to use the judgment, power, and force that they have employed until now. Our police are faced with more and more violence. Often, they are outgunned by the criminals who carry more sophisticated weapons than they carry. Policemen are reflecting the violence they are confronting on a daily basis by becoming more violent and brutal themselves. We are surrounded by a breakdown of law and order.

In the wake of the increasing crime we have experienced, some states have called special sessions of the legislatures to tackle the crime and violence problems. Town meetings, government blue-ribbon panels, and the average man on the street voice their concern and give reasons for the increase in crime. Meanwhile, during all the debate, the drive-by shootings continue and the violence increases. Some of our streets are no longer safe, and many of our communities live with the constant fear of random shootings, gang-related murders, drug dealings, prostitution, general mayhem, intimidation and brutality. Why isn't the average American safe on our urban streets? This questions begs an answer and it certainly points to a crime problem that is out-of-control.

Crimes of random shootings by gangs, are becoming commonplace within our communities. Ethnic gangs are spreading to all major cities. Crime reports implicate younger and younger violators. Gang-related violence is escalating. It appears that a more disproportionate number of crimes are being committed by ethnic members of the underclass. There is developing a distrust and fear of people of color in this country because of the lopsided crime statistics that involve these people.

Our crime statistics concerning murder, rape, arson, and child abuse are getting worse. How can anyone ignore these crime statistics when newspapers, the mass media, and special reports show criminals carousing, loitering, dealing drugs, brutalizing innocent bystanders and admitting to and bragging about other violent activities? Statistics show 1 in every 35 adult males is in some form of correctional facility; 1 in every 9 is an adult black male; of these, 1 in every 4 black males is between 18 and 30 years of age. Today, in the 2000s there is a growing percentage of Hispanics and illegal aliens in our prisons.

The liberal movement insists on turning their heads in denial. They cry racism and make excuses for these criminals and blame their unacceptable behavior on poverty, child abuse, discrimination, poor education, poor job prospects, and many other factors. These criminals are depicted as "victims of society". Is that really the problem? How did society make them victims? Did society prevent them from getting an education when our taxes have supported every conceivable avenue to reach these people? Did society make them victims by granting them free health care in the form of Medicaid? Did society victimize young unmarried mothers by supporting their babies? Did society victimize the ethnic groups by developing affirmative action programs and a quota system? No! Society tried to help. These individuals chose to become victims. Some of the affirmative action programs may have increased criminal behavior by engendering the "I am owed something" mentality. It is interesting that the Washington D.C. area has one of the highest crime rates in America, and the worst child education performance when it receives the most money per child of any city in the U.S.A. No! Money is not the answer.

There comes a time when we must realize that not all people are good. Some individuals are evil, mean, and vicious. No matter how one treats them, they continue to act badly. These people may function normally in civil society when everything goes their way, but lose the veneer of civility when they don't get their way.

These people are lacking self-discipline and self-control. They do not have a conscience or an inner accountability. The concepts of self-discipline and self-control would suggest that a person is inherently good and civil. History does not substantiate this inner goodness of people. In fact, the civility of men, and the lawful behavior amongst men, is prompted and encouraged by the ever-present threat of punishment for lawless behavior.

Historical accounts document that many people will break the law if no one is watching them. Natural disasters, such as hurricane Andrew and the recent Indonesian tsunami disaster, depict dramatic increases in looting, robbery, and other violent crimes by both good and bad individuals. Past history reveals sudden increases in crime during police strikes. Without the threat of punishment many people revert to more primitive behavior. Witness the tragic escalation of crime and violence that occurred in Croatia, Serbia, and Bosnia after the Russian police force was removed. There is something to be said for police presence as a deterrent.

Becoming part of a mob reduces the threat of punishment. Many law-abiding citizens commit violent crimes during union strikes and race riots because of their immunity from punishment as part of the mob, not necessarily because they are evil, uncivilized people. Most retreat from their criminal behavior as soon as the police arrive and there is a threat of punishment. Without the presence of the police to enforce laws, and the threat of punishment for breaking laws, crime increases and we see anarchy and total lawlessness.

As citizens cry for removal of criminals from the streets, and an increase in our police forces to combat these thugs, we are confronted with another obstacle which hampers the efforts of citizens and police officers—the judicial system. The courts will not allow any real punishment of convicts. The closest thing to punishment for crimes committed is being locked up with hoodlum associates, a roof overhead, free medical care, three square meals a day, a gymnasium with all the latest equipment, color television, free education up to obtaining a college degree, and all the civil and prisoner rights that the courts can guarantee. Prisoners have access to better law libraries within their prisons than the average lawyer has in his law office.

The courts are soft on offenders and grant probation to criminals that should be locked away. Our judicial system often imposes sentences that make a mockery out of justice. They allow early parole for hardened criminals. Everyday one hears of chronic criminals being paroled and turned out onto the streets to commit more violent crimes.

Our courts are backlogged and we see prosecuting attorneys and judges encourage plea bargains and reduce sentences to meaningless probation and community service. We see overcrowded prisons and the courts calling for the early release of convicts because there are more and more criminals and not enough prison space. These judges and prosecutors return criminals to the streets because there is no room for them in jails, prisons, and correctional facilities. This practice puts the criminals back into the community, takes the teeth out of the law and encourages even more crime. The criminals have beaten the system and taken advantage of it. Who is in control? Who is responsible?

The welfare state and the entitlement programs along with affirmative action mandates have helped to develop and nurture a permanent underclass. The welfare state was given a big send-off by President Lyndon B. Johnson with his "War on Poverty". Many individuals were, and still are, offered assistance because of their situations and have only taken advantage of the system instead of using it as a bridge to a better life. The intent was commendable but, the results have been disastrous. We have lost the "War on Poverty". In the process, we have become burdened by a criminal underclass looking for handouts. We now have welfare families of three and four generations.

Aid to Families with Dependent Children (AFDC), food stamps, housing allowances, medical care, and educational benefits have assisted in sustaining a large underclass of single-parent families. The single-parent mother is predominantly poverty-stricken. This is witnessed in the underclass community. When AFDC initially began, a high percentage of black babies were born to single mothers. Today almost 70% of all black babies are born to single, unwed mothers. These same programs have fostered a threefold increase in white illegitimacy rates. Today, a high percentage of all white babies are born to single mothers. These programs do not discriminate because of race. Not surprisingly, is the fact that a large percentage of criminals are products of the single-parent family.

The black community was making great strides in the post-WWII years from 1945 to 1965. Illegitimacy was stable at one-third of today's rate. Black prosperity was climbing. The incidence of crime and criminal conviction was on the decline. The rate of educational achievement and the test score disparity between blacks and whites was narrowing. Charles Murray, in his book *Losing Ground,* gives an unbiased, scholarly account of the progress made by blacks from the 1940s through 1965. However, since 1965 and the enactment of the Great Society programs, there has been a reversal of black academic gains, a frightening increase in illegitimacy, and a staggering increase in the percentage of violent crimes committed by blacks.

The entitlement, welfare, and civil rights programs that sounded so compassionate and so well-meaning have failed to produce the desired results. They were created to help the underclass and have only added to the problem. As an example, the AFDC program helped break up the black family by replacing the father and husband with a government subsidy.

Yes, we must admit that our liberal social programs have failed—failed in every area. Medicare and Medicaid have caused increases in medical costs beyond our wildest dreams. Government programs for the homeless have not reduced the homeless problem. Head Start, that lofty sounding program that was supposed to elevate the literacy level of the underclass, has not been translated into higher levels of achievement for the target groups. We have "dumbed down" much of the academic standards so that certain targeted groups can obtain passing grades and become eligible for higher education and advancement. Test performance and academic achievement have been declining with respect to the groups Head Start intended to help. Our politicians point out that these results only mean we need to throw more money into the programs and thus, at the problems. Washington, D.C. here we go again.

These programs all sound so good—but do they really work? The more money we make available for welfare, the more hands there will be to accept the welfare gift. However, many misuse the original intent of the programs. Our entitlement programs have been very successful in creating an underclass of welfare recipients. They have created governmental dependency and have permanently entrenched an entitlement subculture. The entitlement programs are sucking the very life from Americans and the American dream.

The majority of the welfare and entitlement programs are expensive programs that don't work. They comprise more than 50% of our national budget. Consider this: Each working American has to work at least five months out of the year to pay their income taxes—since entitlement programs are more than 50% of the national budget—each taxpayer is working a minimum of two and a half months out of the year for welfare recipients!

The welfare state, though well-intentioned, has damaged the American character. Traditional American values are being eroded and our educational institutions are failing. We glorify *Murphy Brown* and crucify spokesmen for the church, the family, and the moral lifestyle. The Democrats, during the 1992 presidential campaign, made fun of Vice-President Dan Quayle for his support of family values. We are becoming a people without strong beliefs and without strong values. We are becoming a people with a fuzzy understanding of right and wrong. We are becoming a more lenient and less law-abiding country. We have sown the seeds of our own disintegration and we are now frightened of the crime and violence that stalks our streets. We need to change the way we look at crime and the way we treat people convicted of crimes.

New-age reformers and liberals, who say that punishment does not reduce crime or help insure compliance with laws, disregard the facts. Criminals on the streets behave rigidly to rules and regulations imposed upon them by the crime syndicate and gangs. They respect these codes of conduct and behave accordingly, or else. They know that if they "cross-the-line", they will be punished; possibly killed. Thus, it is fair to say: Criminals understand punishment.

Once behind bars, the gang culture still exists with its various hierarchies controlling most prisoners. It has become very evident in the correctional systems that gangs are a powerful force in our prisons. Ethnic gangs now control much of the atmosphere and the behavior within many of our prisons. New prisoners soon learn that they must obey the gang rules or be subject to beatings, sodomy, food restriction, and possible death. It is well-known that some gangsters have maintained control over their previous gangs on the streets from within the prison walls.

The prisons are full of mean-spirited people and the system fails when it tries to rehabilitate them. These prisoners may function in a rigid system with strict discipline such as you might find in a prison, but they are never fully rehabilitated and ready to be turned loose on society. Yet, administrative officials continue to employ the same worn-out versions of failed practices with criminals. We need a new approach and a different outlook to the rehabilitation programs and their problems.

Our prisons allow prisoners many freedoms and opportunities despite the fact they are supposedly being punished in prison. Inmates have work programs, educational opportunities, exercise and sports programs, religious associations, social and psychological counseling, and many more "rehabilitative" programs. Nearly all the comforts of home are available to the convicts: they can write letters; make and receive phone calls; watch television and movies; visit with outsiders;

buy various items; and function almost normally within the prison walls. They have no worries about housing, medical care, and from where their next meal is coming. Despite the normalizing of prison conditions, or perhaps because of it, recidivism remains high and the violence continues. We are doing something wrong.

The rehabilitative efforts offered prisoners are proving to be noneffective when one considers the recidivism rate of criminals returning to society. This relapse into criminal ways seems to be the norm after release from confinement and is often associated with more violent behavior. It would appear that the rehabilitative efforts, the weight training and exercise programs have produced a more violent ruffian. Criminals learn that crime pays. In prison they have the ability to hone their wayward skills and think extensively how they will use them more effectively when they are outside the prison walls. No wonder the penitentiaries are looked upon as graduate schools for criminals.

One may ask, why have our efforts to rehabilitate criminals failed so miserably? Could it be that we all so want the prodigal son to return home again that we totally overlook the failings and mistakes of the system? Whatever the reason, we must admit that the present system of incarceration and rehabilitation is not working. In terms of results, nothing could be less productive than the current programs. We need to realize our failure and reach out for another approach to the problems. It is time for a long overdue change.

The first step in regaining control over our communities in the war against crime is to control our liberal courts and judges who think prisoners deserve more protected rights than the law-abiding citizens. Conviction of a crime should immediately remove certain rights from the convict. I am not advocating cruel and unusual punishment. There should; however, be some form of punishment and some privileges taken away from the lawbreakers. Without the reduction in rights and privileges and without punishment, there would be no reason to obey the law—much the situation we are witnessing today. If we can not control our liberal judges we are doomed to be controlled by the criminal element.

The majority of law-abiding, taxpaying Americans are getting tired of watching the circus being played out in our courtrooms across our country. The time involved and the tax money spent is appalling. Defense lawyer antics and pleadings have made a mockery out of our justice system. We are getting tired of spending so much of our money on our criminal system. A system that has many flaws and does almost nothing to deter crime. A system whose very name, justice system, is a misnomer since it doesn't dispense justice.

Americans are growing weary of politicians swearing to fight crime by putting symbolism over substance. Liberal lawmakers blame society, guns, poverty, racism, and whatever else is "politically correct" as the cause of crime. Instead of buckling down on criminals and holding them accountable for their crimes, the lawmakers are trying to disarm the populace. First, they will force us to register our guns, and later they will confiscate our guns. They hide their true agenda by stating this legislation is aimed at criminals. Really? How many criminals are going to register their guns? Criminals do not abide by the law. They are not going to register their firearms! The only people who will gain by gun registration will be the government; their power over the populace will be greatly increased.

Nowhere in the Second Amendment did our Founding Fathers state, or limit, the right to bear arms. The Second Amendment does not grant the right of arms to be used for hunting and sporting purposes. No, my friends, the Founding Fathers included the right to bear arms expressly for the purpose of defending ourselves against an overly ambitious government. The right to bear arms was the right to shoot people, not animals, who were attempting to limit or reduce our freedom. Every nation throughout history that has lost its freedom and fallen to tyranny, had to disarm the citizens by first confiscating their guns. Exactly what we are seeing today. Isn't it amazing that the country that demands that every household have a gun, Switzerland, has the lowest crime rates in the world.

We need to face the facts. Our judicial system and the court proceedings are on the wrong track for protecting the citizens and punishing the criminals. General consensus agrees that prisons are to punish. Since our current prison system is not producing the results we want, let's change the system. A private business can not keep losing money on failed programs and products; if they do, they go bankrupt. Our government has the money, let's spend it more wisely.

A worthwhile consideration for a change in the present correctional programs is the intelligent use of isolation. Whenever isolation is mentioned; the courts, the prisoners, and the liberal correctional philosophy think of it as "cruel and unusual punishment". Current penal practice uses isolation only for the most difficult and destructive inmates. They think a convict who is isolated will lose his mind; however, the facts do not substantiate their fears.

Hostages Donald Sutherland and Terry Anderson, who were captives in Iran, Sen John McCain, a Vietnam prisoner, many other P.O.W.s, and countless noncriminals have endured isolation and torture and none of them have "lost their minds". To the contrary, they all seem to place a higher value on their freedom and living peacefully. Many of these ex-prisoners and hostages are on speaking tours extolling the higher value of life; there is not an idiot among them. We are constantly being told that if we isolate these tough prisoners, that we will cause them psychological damage and ruin their lives. This simply is not the case.

I have been in isolation; albeit, not to the extent or the duration of our famous hostages or P.O.W.s. It happened in the fall of 1949 when I was in the Marine Corps. I was stationed at Marine Barracks, Agana, Guam. I was the only Pfc—private first class—that was going to be promoted to the grade of Corporal—a big deal in the Marine Corps in 1949.

Two friends and I left our quonset hut, went down through the jungle, and went swimming in the lagoon as a pre-promotion celebration. We were not on official liberty. We were swimming for about 50 minutes. As we headed back to our station, we realized that we might be late for bed check. We did what any good Marine would do—ran as fast as we could through the main gate and did not stop until we were back in our quonset hut. Shortly thereafter, the officer of the day came through the hut and told us we had missed bed check. We would have to stand for a hearing in front of the commander in the morning.

The next morning I was all pressed and polished for my hearing in front of the Colonel: The crusty, old Colonel that led the Marines ashore at Iwo Jima in 1945. While standing at rigid attention, I noticed that there were other officers in the room standing at attention. I thought to myself—all this pomp and ceremony for 50 minutes swimming—and I broke out laughing! The Colonel was red-faced and furious. I could not stop laughing. He ordered me to be taken out and court martialed.

I was sentenced to 30 days bread and water in solitary confinement. Solitary confinement in a four-foot by eight-foot cell with no mattress, no chair, and no personal effects got my attention. The thing I remember most about my sentence was the bread and water part. Guam is a warm, humid island and all my bread had weevils crawling in it. I think I survived the ordeal.

Nine months later, I made the Inchon landing with the 1st Marine Division and later fought my way out of the Chosin Reservoir surrounded by 300,000 Chinese. I graduated from the University of Colorado in 1956 and taught high school for one year. Subsequently, I went to medical school and obtained my M.D. degree in 1961. I am still practicing medicine in Colorado. I can add my name to other people who have survived the ordeal of isolation and am no worse off because of the experience. It was an ordeal that makes one think.

It is because of my experience with isolation that I know it can be a very useful tool in the treatment and rehabilitation of criminals. Isolation is the most important first step in this new prison reform and rehabilitation program. Isolation, coupled with other innovative rehabilitative techniques will work. In the Iso-Rehab plan each prisoners' cell or unit is an isolation module. It is constructed and managed to make the prisoner dependent on the retraining process. Prisoners in their cell units are not subservient or controlled by the prison gang leader, the prison hierarchy, or the threat of sexual and bodily harm. Iso-Rehab can alter criminal behavior and rehabilitate.

The actual rehabilitation-retraining program of the Iso-Rehab system, presented herein, relies on psychological and mental reconditioning. In general, all learning is psychological and mental dependent. The mind is the only human function than can be educated and trained. Some critics may argue that Iso-Rehab is "brainwashing" prisoners. If brainwashing connotes cleaning and removing the evil thoughts from a criminals' mindset, so be it. If brainwashing facilitates retraining, reforming, and rehabilitating, all the better.

The psychological methods employed in the Iso-Rehab system, is suggestive psychological retraining, not brainwashing. The Iso-Rehab program allows the prisoner to reach his own conclusions, from suggestions about behavior and the proper behavior acceptable in the community at large. If these suggestions are not incorporated into the prisoners' thinking and lifestyle, then the prisoner may fail to become rehabilitated. Compared to the miserable failure rate of rehabilitation in our current penal systems, the Iso-Rehab system brings new hope.

The present breed of criminologists and rehabilitation experts are part of a multibillion dollar government corporation and would balk at the suggestions and methods of housing and controlling convicted criminals proposed in *Alone to Think*. Speaking from their lofty perch of prison enlightenment and reform, they may denounce these ideas as a step backward in the penal system. But, these methods hold a promise for revision and renewal that is long overdue. Weak methods have been employed for years. To continue these failing methods would be most dangerous, especially when one realizes that the great experiment to rehabilitate criminals has been tried, implemented, and failed. Few, if any, criminals are "rehabilitated" enough to return to normal productive lives. Most of the ex-cons go through revolving doors and eventually return to prison—the recidivism rates prove this.

Reforming the penitentiary system is worth consideration and will be found to be both economically enticing and psychologically stimulating. An old cliche says "we pay for what we value". Therefore, at an average annual price of $30,000.00 or more per inmate, and much more for "lifers" and prisoners on death row, we must value our prisoners. Penitentiaries have become very expensive and staffing them with rehabilitation programs and personnel is economically prohibitive— the correctional system is a multibillion dollar per year expense. It is indeed time to consider a new approach. We need to restructure our present prison facilities and implement new methods of rehabilitation that work. Perhaps then we can release a productive member back into society who is ready to take on the responsibility of living a better life. Americans are resourceful and can realize mistakes and cure the disease of crime that they have neglected. Time is of the essence and action needs to be taken now.

In the event that the Iso-Rehab system fails to rehabilitate a prisoner, there are still many advantages that outweigh the current system.

1. No crime and criminal training will have taken place in the Iso-Rehab units.

2. The prison, as the graduate school for criminals would have been eliminated.

3. Prisoners would be safe from bodily harm.

4. Prisoners would be safe from sexual abuse.

5. AIDS transmission would be cut to zero.

6. Maintenance of ties to criminal gangs and organizations would be eliminated.

7. Cost savings would be significant.

8. Iso-Rehab will make all prisoners, no matter how tough and vicious, think about themselves, their futures, and their behavior.

9. The Iso-Rehab facility is a cost-effective way to get offenders off the streets.

10. The Iso-Rehab system eliminates addictions to alcohol, tobacco, and drugs by simply stopping the use of these addicting agents.

There are many more reasons that would favor the Iso-Rehab type of penal rehabilitation over our current correctional institutions. If a proposal seems strange, think of the current systems' counterpart that is now failing. Weigh the good against the bad—is it better to be isolated and safe or to be raped and beaten etc., etc.? Contrary to current authorities, we can prevent the brutality of our current system. We can house all of our criminals. We can keep them for the full term of their sentence. We can save money. We might actually be able to deter crime and rehabilitate criminals. Prison reform with isolation may be the first step toward curing the crime problem in America.

Since the Iso-Rehab prison is a new concept, and has a better rehabilitation possibility, the initial term of confinement could be reduced. Therefore, if a term of ten years was given for a certain crime in our present prison system, a reduction to perhaps five years in the Iso-Rehab would be sufficient.

Chapter Two

Punishment and Confinement

Historical View of Prison as Punishment

Numerous books have been written on the history of prisons, punishment, and confinement. This brief historical perspective is offered only as a brief explanation and overview. Why are there prisons in the first place? First and foremost, prisons were originally established to punish the wrong-doers. Universally, society has condemned and defined violent acts that harm citizens and society as criminal behavior. Punishment was prescribed for crimes and criminal activity. Public whippings, mutilations, brandings, stocks, pillories and even death were various forms of punishment.

The first U.S. prison was built in 1787 on Walnut Street in Philadelphia, Pennsylvania. Criminals were sent to this prison and worked hard without pay. This hard work and no pay was referred to as retribution or just deserts, and was supposed to be a deterrent for criminal activity. The Quakers helped pass laws that made labor the punishment for crime. Prisoners were made to perform slave labor. This form of labor-intensive punishment helped build the pyramids of Egypt and the Aztec structures of Central America. Punishment and slave labor also assisted in the building of the Great Wall of China.

Criminals also were defined by the people who enjoyed the preponderance of power at the time. A criminal could be defined as a politician with contrary views; hence political prisoners. A criminal could be defined as a debtor; hence the origin of the debtor prison. These prisons or workhouses were created so that dead beats could work off their debts performing labor. Various forms of industrial prisons have been around in our U.S.A. since the mid-1800s. Some vestiges of industrial prison activity still exists as prisoners today maintain farms, manufacture license plates, and fashion prison-made products, such as jute sacks, furniture, clothing and various products too numerous to mention.

The history of incarcerating criminals is as old as civilization. Throughout the world, society has demanded that violent criminals be incarcerated. Various groups, tribes, countries, and empires have incarcerated lesser people and criminal types. The Quakers believed that criminals would benefit from penance and so the term "penitentiary" was born.

Reformatories were developed to help the young criminals to "reform" their errant ways that were caused by their environment. Such factors as poverty and the association of bad influences were thought to be causes of their crimes. The youthful offenders were removed from society and "rehabilitated". As time passed, overcrowding of jails and penitentiaries became a major problem which led to brutal behavior of prisoners toward one another, to the guards, and the guards toward the prisoners.

Incarceration and enslavement of people as a means of punishment is a well-established human tradition. These traditional methods serve several purposes:

1. Removes the criminal from society thereby making the citizens safer and more secure;

2. Provides a cheap source of labor;

3. Acts as a form of punishment that helps to deter crime; and

4. Stands as a warning signal to citizens that they should obey the law.

Over the years, prisons and incarceration existed to protect society, to provide an element of force for our laws, and to warn lawbreakers of the rewards for disobedience to the laws. The thought of treating prisoners as victims who need treatment and rehabilitation is of rather recent origin. The implementation of our penal reform and rehabilitative programs have witnessed a concomitant rise in recidivism, increased crime rates, and disrespect for the law.

Confinement of Criminals to Protect Society

Peaceful communities have always defined criminal behavior as a threat to their security and continued existence. Securing a safe community is paramount in our urban and high-density centers where workers must leave their homes and travel to the workplace. We need safe streets, neighborhoods, and a safe environment in which to work and produce the goods that ensure a viable America. We need safe communities in which to live and raise our children. We cannot function if we have a constant worry concerning our safety. Drive-by shootings, gang murders, and drug dealings erode our neighborhoods. We cannot be productive members of society if we are threatened on our streets and homes by criminals. Thus, the need to remove the criminals from our communities is becoming more important to ensure our safety.

Removing the criminals from the "normal" or law-abiding community serves two very important functions. First, it helps to exclude, as did quarantining for infectious disease, an element or factor that can weaken and prey upon a host: the law-abiding community. Second, by separating, through incarceration or imprisonment, it stands or serves as an example to remind the law-abiding society to obey the law or suffer the consequences. The need to segregate and incarcerate criminals is more important today than at any time in our history.

Prisons and prisoner confinement are tools of society that can be used to insure the safe and efficient existence of society. Confinement means: to limit, to restrict, and to restrain. To be effective and safe, confinement should provide for the safety and security of the convicts as well as the community. The current practices of confinement in the U.S. does neither of these.

Prisoners in today's prisons are subject to possible beatings by other prisoners and brutalized by prison gangs. They can be sodomized by degenerate and sexually perverted convicts.

At one prison the term "gay", which was used to describe homosexuality was changed to "SAD" by the inmates. This was done because they realized that the word "gay" meant happy, joyous, and lighthearted. The prison inmates knew that homosexuals were anything but gay, happy, and lighthearted. They called them "SADS' which stood for sodomites and degenerates — the inmates thought this was a more realistic description of the homosexuals.

Prisoners should be restrained and segregated not only from our communities but also from one another. The inmates are not safe from one another and the evil that is prevalent within our prisons. The statistics of crimes committed in prisons to fellow inmates is overwhelming. Beatings, rapes, thefts, and murder is rampant. Being incarcerated does not insure one's security from the criminal activity that is bred and fostered within our prisons. Released prisoners who commit more violent crimes reflect the schooling they have obtained while behind bars. Recidivists are generally sentenced for more serious crimes after their prison experience.

Something is wrong with our current system of confinement if both the prisoners and the communities are not improved after the experience of prison confinement. If our present system is supposed to protect the community and "rehabilitate" the criminal, then we are being shortchanged by a very costly program that does not work.

All is not lost. We should not throw-the-baby-out-with-the-bath-water. Systems need periodic evaluation, revision, and fine-tuning to insure optimum performance. However, faulty judicial thinking and liberal agendas have been allowed to render a worthwhile and useful tool—prison confinement—almost worthless. With a little fine-tuning, our present system can be "rehabilitated" and perform as originally intended.

Chapter Three

Role of the Judicial System

Punishment and the Judicial System

Our legal system has confused the entire issue of crime and punishment. From the first moment the accused comes into contact with the judicial process there is confusion. An arresting officer is not allowed to accept a voluntary confession for fear of encroaching on an individuals' Miranda Rights. These rights protect an offender against self-incrimination. This confuses wrong-doers who may want to get the criminal act off their chest and get on with the punishment they deserve. The message comes across that the judicial system does not really want the accused to be guilty and punished until the courtroom game is played out.

Many judges, to safeguard an offenders' rights, would rather accept a "not guilty" plea so that the game can be drawn out to its final conclusion despite all the time, energy, and money that is required in this attempt. This gives a criminal the message that the concept known as justice, along with the judicial process, is a game that one can play, and with the right players and strategy, probably win.

In the judicial arena the goal or prize of winning this game is the reduction or negation of punishment. If the defense lawyers play the game well, the accused receives a reduced sentence and milder punishment. The message that is given is that a good lawyer can win the courtroom game and frustrate justice. Our judicial system has forgotten that justice is supposed to deal with truth, law, and order. This confusion invariably alters the effects of punishment for unacceptable behavior.

The current form of imprisonment as punishment for crimes does not work—or does not work very well. The reason that punishment or the threat of punishment returns less than expected results in America, is due to the judicial process used in handling criminal suspects. This is directly related to the extensive time delay from the criminal act and the punishment for the act. To be an effective deterrent for crime, punishment must be expedient and specific. A person caught in the act of committing a crime should be punished immediately. This is not the case in our present system. Our current judicial agenda causes this delay because it places more value on protecting criminal rights than on the rights of law-abiding citizens.

Today, not only is the judicial process slow to punish, but we see punishment that does not equate with the wrongful act. In order for justice to be served, the punishment should fit the crime committed. Punishment that is delayed by the legal system and does not fit the offense loses its importance as an educational tool and does not act as a deterrent for further criminal activity.

Time-worn educational theory emphasizes that punishment or praise must follow an act immediately to be effective. The quicker the praise or punishment, the greater the educational value of the reward or correction. Only an idiot touches a red hot stove two times in close succession. We don't have to ask why. We know that when we touch a hot stove we get burned. The punishment is immediate and is indelibly impressed upon us. We touch a hot stove, we burn our finger, lesson learned: We do not touch hot stoves.

The juvenile court system, which was originally conceived as a compassionate means of dealing with immature miscreants, has fostered several generations of adult criminals. The juvenile court, which took the position of the national parent of neglected, youthful offenders, has championed treatment and reformation of wayward, criminal youths rather than punishment for crimes they committed. This attitude of leniency for criminal acts, which started in the U.S. in the early 1800s, has gradually permeated the entirety of judicial and correctional thought.

Many of the ills that we find today in our justice and correctional programs can be directly attributed to this leniency philosophy. We have become soft on crime and look for excuses that caused the offenders to express themselves in a criminal way. We, the courts and the judicial system as the national parent, blame ourselves and society for not providing a better atmosphere in which to raise our children and thereby prevent their falling into crime.

Our mass media, the daily newspapers, and TV, are continuously telling us that poor education and crime are caused by poverty and the fact that we are not providing enough money and support for the poor. I don't believe this.

Immediately after the Vietnam war many Vietnamese came to America. The Vietnamese parents could often be seen walking our streets carrying plastic garbage bags on their shoulders supported by a broom stick — they were poor — very poor, and they collected aluminum cans for money to help support themselves. However, their children excelled in our schools and many were at the top of their respective high school classes — despite being very poor. This situation has changed. The second and third generations of these same immigrants have succumbed to our welfare mentality. We now have Asian gangs and Asian criminal activity which has replaced the Asian mom and pop aluminum can collectors.

The research has been completed and the facts are out. The consensus of opinion based upon the results of thousands of juvenile criminal case studies flatly state:

1. Leniency for juvenile offenders sends them the wrong message: the law is impotent;

2. If one allows a child to go unpunished for bad behavior, the child will continue the bad behavior;

3. Harsher punishment for criminal behavior results in less recidivism;

4. The sooner juveniles are punished for crimes, the better the chance the youths will have to break the crime habit; and

5. At-home surveillance, soft probation, and coddling of youthful criminals only breeds contempt for laws and

the justice system and fosters lives of crime.

So it is, that the miscreant, the thug, the hoodlum, and all criminals in general, become themselves, the victims of society. The belief that society, and not the criminal, is responsible for crime has been the undoing of our judicial, correctional, and rehabilitation systems. This reasoning denies the role of punishment in the correctional process and substitutes instead, an attitude that coddling and compassionate support will solve our crime problem.

The failure to prescribe early and adequate sanctions on criminal behavior only fosters more crime. The failure to remove the youthful offender from the environment that nurtured the misbehavior is a mistake that goes against all principles of psychology with regards to learning. Juvenile courts and judges who allow, yeah even insist, that juvenile offenders stay at home in their communities to be disciplined and retrained are guilty of faulty reasoning and are themselves part of the growing crime problem in this country. There is overwhelming evidence that early apprehension, appropriate punishment, and isolation by way of incarceration, is an effective, albeit not 100%, way to control and correct criminal behavior.

The maturation process, along with sequestration, becomes a prime factor in the control and reduction of criminal activity. We find very few elderly individuals involved in violent crime. In fact, the ex-governor of Colorado, Richard Lamm, stated flatly that the only thing that helps crime is the maturation and aging of convicts. He was dismayed, as are most thinking citizens, by the dismal statistics of our rehabilitation efforts. It is imperative that we review our entire process of handling, punishing, and rehabilitating our criminals. The protection of our communities and the preservation of our country demands no less.

The legal system today has various methods routinely used by attorneys to benefit their clients. They include plea bargaining and concurrent sentencing for more than one crime. Also used is the appeal process which may extend and delay the final sentencing of their clients almost indefinitely. The attorneys can also ensure that their clients can use the bail system if desired. This process may put the criminals back out on the streets. The parole system can obviate the effect of the sentence and the punishment.

The routine judicial proceedings may be as follows; A "not-guilty" plea is entered and usually a long lapse of time passes before a trial ensues. Once in court, the defense uses many tactics, including lies and misinformation, to confuse and cloud the issue of guilt for the crime. The defense tries to drag the trial out as long as possible. This gives the defense time to caress the defendant and makes the jury see the offender as a "normal" person. The defense tries to persuade the jury that each of them may have acted as the defendant did if their situations were the same. Child abuse, poverty, parental neglect, racism, and other societal pressures "forced" the defendant's behavior. If the defense can confuse the case enough to sway the jury, the wrong-doer may be found not guilty and returned back into the community.

The defense also coaches the accused on what to wear, how to sit, and how to act. Making eye contact with certain jurors is another defense strategy for the criminal. Having the accused voice concern and feel compassion for the victim often sways the jury and sometimes softens the judges' sentence. Making the accused look like a normal family member makes a pitch to the jury—there but for the grace of God go I.

If the plea bargain method is used, the case may be settled sooner, but the punishment is so reduced as to have no impact on the offender. By reducing the sentence through a plea bargain, the punishment becomes more acceptable in the eyes of the criminal. The plea bargain process, used routinely today, has reduced punishment to a bargaining chip—a license to violate the law.

Judge Ralph Adam Fine, in his book *Escape of the Guilty* gives numerous examples of how the plea bargaining practice employed by most courts has reduced punishment to a commodity. Punishment as less of a threat, is bargained away for the expediency of reducing the courts' case load. The very nature of the plea bargain encourages a guilty plea to a lesser crime. Thus, a reduced or more lenient verdict diminishes the impact of the law. According to Judge Fine, the impact of punishment as a deterrent is decreased.

The plea bargain process encourages a suspect to plead guilty to a lesser crime that the accused may not be guilty of committing. This practice becomes a hoax. It allows the accused to be sentenced for a crime that he or she did not commit. This gives some credence to the prisoners lament that they are "not guilty". They are being sentenced for a crime they did not commit.

When the reduction in punishment is coupled with the practice of serving time concurrently for several crimes committed—usually for the lesser of the crimes—it has the effect of no punishment at all for the more serious crimes. Plea bargaining, in the criminals' mind, has become the cost of doing business. Criminals know this, as do defense attorneys, who consider all the options to get the "best deal" for the criminal during the trial and sentencing debacle. The criminals brag about the deal acquired through the plea bargaining process.

In the event the jury finds the accused guilty, the appeal process may be used to overturn the verdict and probably mitigate the eventual sentencing and punishment. The appeal process may require another trial and further delay. This whole process is long drawn-out, very expensive, and has very little, if any, educational and deterrent effect on the guilty party. Moreover, the criminal comes away with the feeling that I-can-beat-the-system-next-time.

Another factor to be considered in reducing the deterrent effect of punishment is the parole system. Amazing as it may seem, many prisoners who have long criminal records and who may be serving a ten-to-twenty year sentence, may be eligible for parole within six months. All the prisoner has to do is show the proper "reformed" attitude and obey the rules: don't make waves. Also, criminals discover very early in their careers that the appearance of remorse, the adoption of religion, and a few well-chosen "I'm sorry" words, can sway a judge and jury in the trial and the sentencing procedure, as well as during the parole review board.

Sometimes the legal system will totally dismiss charges against a criminal if the guilty person will help the prosecution track down and arrest others or possibly solve a case. This is known as granting immunity from prosecution and translates into less punishment even though the cooperating criminal is guilty of a crime. Many criminals can bargain for a lesser sentence and be charged with lesser offenses if they "turn state evidence". Being granted immunity by turning state evidence goes hand-in-hand with plea bargaining. Both these practices work to weaken the legal system and the effect of punishment.

All of these factors: the delay in the trial process; plea bargaining; concurrent sentencing; being a witness for the state; remorse for the crime—for being caught; and the defense attorneys' attempt to make the criminal look like a victim of society, reduce the threat of punishment for a crime. Is there any wonder why American criminologists feel that punishment has no deterrent value for criminal activity?

The rehabilitation movement of the penal system and criminologists flatly state that punishment does little to deter crime. However, they overlook the systems that do work. The recidivism of Japanese convicts is only a fraction of ours. Japanese prisons are no picnic and prisoners do not want to return to them. Singapore, lying directly in the middle of the golden drug triangle, has almost zero drug crime. Dealing drugs in Singapore is punishable by hanging. There is no confusion. One does not deal drugs in Singapore. The punishment is well understood and is a successful deterrent.

We wonder why we are told punishment is no deterrent for criminal behavior. Punishment and praise can be effective as deterrents to crime, but they must be used properly and timely. The entire legal-judicial process, as it stands now, confuses the issues of what is a crime, who is or is not guilty, and what penalty, if any, should be given. No wonder our present system is in a quandary. Our present judicial system needs to change if it is to have any effect on crime occurrence, crime deterrence, and the rate of recidivism. The time for change is long overdue.

Judges—Aiding and Abetting Crime

Around 1970, something happened to cause the courts to expand their influence and infiltrate almost every aspect of American life. Perhaps the courts became more involved in our lives because they were swayed by the turbulent 1960s and the Civil Rights movement. Perhaps it was the ascendancy of the ACLU and various civil rights groups that demanded constitutional blessings and interpretations of their agendas that fueled the expansion dreams of the court. Perhaps the courts became power hungry and moved into a vacuum that was not filled by another branch of government. Whatever the stimulus for judicial expansion, it is a *fait accompli*.

Today, the tentacles of the court have infiltrated virtually every facet of our lives and have a stranglehold on almost everything we do. The courts control the educational system through their decrees on integration, busing to end segregation, controls of curriculum, ethnic teacher hiring quotas, and laws governing who will have access to the classrooms and what will be allowed therein. The courts have also expanded into the world of business and now influence many aspects of labor and commerce. They dictate guidelines on hiring practices, quotas, sexual harassment, age discrimination and promotions, as well as job termination. The courts have their fingers in the environmental and pollution arenas. They decide which groups are entitled to special rights and protections such as minorities, gays, lesbians, and other special interest groups such as criminals, juveniles, females, the disabled, and religious sects.

Our Founding Fathers, the framers of our Constitution, gave this country a document that spelled out certain rights and put restrictions on government. They restricted the greedy tentacles of government and championed personal freedom and responsibility. The writers of our Constitution would be saddened to see the way our liberal activist jurists bend and twist the intent of the constitution to embrace their agenda. An agenda that places more power in the hands of government and reduces personal freedoms.

If the courts had a hands-off policy concerning prisons prior to the 1970s, they have certainly done a 180 degree turn around. Since 1970 the courts have increased their hands-on approach and now control much of the organization and management of our prisons. This is especially true concerning prisoners rights and the environment within the cell block. The courts have developed "constitutional concerns" regarding prison overcrowding, medical care, educational and work opportunities, continual legal education, food service, safety, and the overall normalization of life behind bars. This judicial hand print can be seen on all aspects of the jail and prison system. Judges now prescribe the "constitutionality" of the conditions within our jails and prisons despite the fact that our Constitution makes no mention of judicial control of prisons.

Since the 1970s more and more prison systems have been forced by judicial decree to "improve' and change. These decrees followed a thirty year period of steady improvement in the quality of prison life from 1940 to 1970—all without the heavy hand of the courts. The judicial system now dictates the entire range of penal conditions. Judges, along with civil rights activists, are focused on "prisoner rights". As the Civil Rights mandates and entitlement programs grew and were nurtured by judicial blessings, so did the rights and entitlements of prisoners. Inmates who victimized thousands of law-abiding citizens and their families were guaranteed many rights when incarcerated. We are being victimized by criminals who attack us and strip us of our rights. However, the courts today seem more concerned with the rights of vicious criminals than with the rights of victims, their families, and our communities. The courts have lost their focus.

Criminals who violate law-abiding citizens should have their rights strictly limited when they enter the confines of prison. Instead, the courts step in and make sure the prisoners are comfortable and conditions are agreeable. They monitor prison conditions and take extra steps to insure that the civil rights of vicious murderers, thieves, and rapists are preserved on the highest level. They don't; however, prevent some prisoners from being sodomized and beaten. They can't control the creation and the operation of prison gangs.

We can ask, 'whose rights should be respected and protected'? Criminals had citizen's rights that they gambled away when they committed crimes. They victimized innocent citizens and must now suffer the consequences. When convicted of crimes, the prisoners should surrender some of the rights they had. That would be justice; but, our justice system—that we support with our tax dollars—victimizes all of us by forcing us to pay and insure that criminals have a comfortable life behind bars. The courts have lost sight of the victims' rights. A judicial system that fights for the rights of the criminal more than the rights and wishes of the law-abiding citizenry is truly confused about justice and the role of the courts as expressed in our Constitution.

Today, virtually all prison systems are monitored, controlled, and labor under the threat of class action suits to protect and extend the rights of prisoners. Judges feel they are helping the criminals by making these changes but, as always, the road to hell is paved with good intentions. These judicial decrees are insulting the true victims who have been violated: the taxpaying, law-abiding citizens.

With the continual improvement of prison life, incarceration does not seem so awful to inmates. The idea of punishment has lost its sting. The hand that is supposed to punish criminals is turning them back onto the streets or housing them comfortably for shorter periods of time. We have witnessed a rapid increase in the rate of crime that has paralleled the increase of judicial encroachment and control of our correctional systems.

One would expect that the tax dollars that support our correctional institutions would "buy" better results when prisoners are released from incarceration. The rehabilitated ex-con should be more civilized after serving time in our 'enlightened' rehabilitative facilities. We are shocked and dismayed when we read statistics that show an increase of repeat offenders and the increase in the overall crime rate. Being incarcerated today allows a prisoner to associate and mingle with many of his old friends and gang members.

The prison has become a post graduate education center where prisoners can learn from one another how to beat the system and possibly not get caught the next time, after they are released. The prison gymnasium and work-out areas are places where prisoners can train and muscle-up for their next criminal adventure.

We get a strong indication that we are merely paying for criminal education and the probability of being victimized repeatedly. Criminals receive a more comfortable life behind bars and taxpayers foot the bill. The only thing we receive for our tax dollars is a feeling of insecurity when we walk the streets. The criminals rob and victimize us in numerous ways and they are aided and abetted by our judges. The judicial mandates that normalize prison life will insure this trend continues. There is need for a change.

Chapter Four

Rehabilitation

Rehabilitation

What is the meaning of rehabilitation? The dictionary defines rehabilitate as:

1. restore to rank, privileges, or property which one has lost;

2. restore the good name or reputation of; reinstate in good repute;

3. put back in good condition, reestablish on a firm, sound basis;

4. bring or restore to a normal or optimum state of health by constructive activity via medical treatment, physical or psychological therapy, vocational counseling and training.

These definitions seem very idealistic when one realizes the number of repeat offenders that fill our prisons, penitentiaries, and correctional institutions today. The failure of prison rehabilitation programs is shown by the high percentage of recidivism and the increasing violence of crimes committed by ex-convicts who have been "rehabilitated". The administration of most prisons continues to justify having expensive rehabilitation programs despite the disastrous results. The rehabilitative-correctional officials who manage these programs ignore the failings and continue to believe that theirs is the truly enlightened way to deal with prisoners. Perhaps a review is in order.

Do Correctional Facilities Really "Correct" Behavior?

Most states call their penal institutions and their prison systems "Department of Corrections". This, as it turns out, is a misnomer. First of all, no one in their right mind, would put a bunch of thugs together in the same facility and think that such a grouping would have salutary effects. Such a combination of malcontents provides only role models who have committed the most heinous crimes. The hierarchy of the convict congregation puts the worst and most violent prisoners at the top. A petty thief could not possibly command as much respect as a multiple ax murderer or serial killer. And so it is, from the very outset, the correctional role of our facilities is doomed to failure. When the worst criminals are afforded the highest ranking and are granted tenure because of their crime accomplishments, they, as role models, give the wrong message to prisoners who might possibly be "corrected" and rehabilitated.

Secondly, to mix first time nonviolent offenders with hardened, violent prison leaders, who are granted respect by their peers is antagonistic to any form of "correction". Prisoners thrown into the general mix of convicts, from minor offenders and petty criminals to big-time, hardened, chronic prisoners, must, out of necessity obey the rules of the convict club and culture. They learn fast because they are being taught by top-notch criminals. They understand punishment.

How can we expect "correction" to take place in a facility that is ruled by the most hardened and tenured thugs? We can't. Correction does not and can not take place under these conditions. A parallel on a different level can be made: sending fresh, new congressmen to Washington D.C. to correct the ills of Congress. The new members soon learn that they must obey the rules and follow the party line. So it is in prisons. No matter how a new prisoner may feel upon entering the facility to start his prison career, he soon learns to behave and accept the prisoners' code of conduct.

A third reason for the failure of our correctional system is the mixing and liberal association of hardened convicts and their influence on less experienced criminals. Mixing prisoners together allows the free flow of ideas and thoughts. This free flow of criminal information helps hone criminal skills. Prisoners can exchange ideas as to how they can possibly beat-the-system next time. The exercise programs and physical fitness courses insure that we have stronger more violent criminals upon their release back into society. This is not rehabilitation as it was meant to be.

A fourth reason for failure is the atmosphere of fear that is currently found in our prisons. A new prisoner is fair game for intimidation, assault, and threats. This overwhelming psychological pressure of the prison gang culture is so strong and pervasive that it stymies any reform or rehabilitation.

Surely, no thinking person would consider such a system to be a treatment for the "correction" of misbehavior. To do so would be like taking an out-of-tune jalopy and trying to compete in the Indianapolis 500: The cards are stacked against you. We find the media concerning us with "prisoners' rights", and the rehabilitation-correctional movement supports these cries of the prisoners and the media. Are the rights of criminals what we really value? Presently, we are supporting and paying for these current systems of correction and rehabilitation. If we value what we pay for, why should we pay for a failing system? Perhaps we are being hoodwinked because any thinking person can realize these flaws in our present systems. We need a change and we need it now.

Who Is to Blame?

A rehabilitation agenda is taught in all schools of criminology and correctional behavior. The rehabilitative movement believes that criminals are a product of their environment. They have succumbed to criminal misconduct because of the pressures of society. Society is at fault for their criminal misbehavior and therefore, responsible for their rehabilitative treatment. Punishment is not in their agenda as an acceptable means of rehabilitation. These criminals have been punished enough by the demands of society. They say it is time to help the victims of society—the criminals. In America today, one could not get through the correctional curriculum if one wasn't thoroughly in step with this rehabilitation agenda of dealing with criminals.

Many experienced correctional authorities proclaim that rehabilitation does not work. Criminologists and correctional officers, who have been trained according to this rehabilitative agenda, are experiencing reality shock as they come to realize that some criminals are just bad, mean-spirited individuals who lack discipline and respect for the law. The rehabilitation and treatment program removes the responsibility for criminal misconduct from an individual who committed the crime and places it elsewhere. By supporting these ill-conceived beliefs it is becoming clear that the rehabilitation movement is closely connected to the "root causes" of crime

Their agenda supports the concept that society is responsible for the criminal behavior. Therefore, society should pay for any rehabilitation necessary to correct the criminals' problem. The rehabilitation movement believes that the "system" failed and so society must reach out and help these criminals. Thus, not only do we have prison rehabilitation programs, but, outside in the communities, agencies are formed to provide care for young criminals-to-be: e.g., Persons in Need of Service (PINS). This philosophy and agenda is well on the way to making the law-abiding, taxpaying citizen responsible for all crimes and criminal activity.

It has become politically correct to view a criminal as a "victim" of any number of factors that caused his criminal behavior. The criminal and the rehabilitative community need to blame someone other than the individual committing the crime. The criminal's behavior is simply a symptomatic expression of the victim's illness. Viewed in this light, is there any wonder why criminals are treated as patients who need care rather than as thugs and hoodlums who should be punished for misbehaving and breaking the law?

So it is that the entire rehabilitation philosophy is to view criminals as victims and patients that need to be treated and cured of their disease. The entire reform agenda considers any prisoner able to be cured by a rehabilitation program. Once the criminal is healed, or cured of the illness of "criminal behavior", a return to normal behavior within the community is expected and accepted. But this is not happening.

The question of why some individuals become criminals and others do not has yet to be answered. We know that some people obey the law and others do not. The causes of crime present the chicken-or-the-egg argument. Which comes first? Crime and criminal activity causing poverty? Or does poverty have a role in causing crime? Many poverty-stricken countries have very low crime rates, and some affluent countries have high crime rates. We know that criminal activity can weaken a society and its efforts to become productive and thus cause poverty. However, this same reasoning and argument can be used to disprove any cause of crime.

The rehabilitation movement is fueled by the reasoning that society is responsible for criminal behavior. They blame multiple factors in society as the cause of criminals' behavior. These factors run the gamut from poverty, racism, ethnic origin, lack of education, environment, and any other cause that the movement might favor. These societal pressures caused, and therefore, justify the criminals acting unacceptably within the communities. This thinking is used to excuse the criminals' failure to become civilized and responsible along with their refusal to accept and live by the norms and laws of civilized, peaceful communities. Offenders lament, society-did-this-to-me. We have taken the responsibility for crime away from the criminal and put it on the community, the school system, the state, and the country.

Modern society is being drawn away from a morally sound and productive environment by this type of thinking formulated within the liberal movement. No longer is an individual held accountable and responsible for his behavior. No longer is he to be expected to conform to rules and laws established long ago and proven effective over time. No longer is he encouraged to learn all he can to better himself and strive for the best. Instead, he is taught that by merely "being", he is entitled to certain privileges that up until recently others had to work hard for and earn. Modern psychological thinking suggests that people deserve certain status and privileges whether they earn them or not.

Today, as a result of the civil rights movement, certain groups demand more than equal opportunity. They demand equal results and equal outcomes without earning the outcome by equal performance. Even in the school environment, nonperforming children are passed without regard to performance, so that they can "feel good" about themselves. This is window dressing and resembles equal opportunity, but in reality it allows equal results for unequal performance. This is discrimination, but the liberal agenda blurs it by saying it is equal opportunity. They feel that children deserve the right to gain the prize of a passing grade even if they did not earn it.

This is witnessed in other realms of the work force as well as in schools. It is misleading and wrong.

The modern educational system is being affected by this same thought process. Today, if a juvenile does not go to school and learn the basic education offered in society, and does not learn to act according to the laws that govern acceptable behavior, it is the fault of the school and the community. The entire education program in the U.S. has become closely linked to the need to have students feel good about themselves instead of pushing themselves to learn all they can and strive to excel in the basics presented. Modern psychological thinking contends that many criminals did not feel good about themselves and did not strive to learn while in school and turned to crime to gain respect and a feeling of personal power. This suggests it is not the individual who fails to make the grade, but the school system that fails to teach the student meaningful material. The school placed too many demands on the student and caused him not to feel good about himself.

The psychological community rationalizes all forms of deviant behavior by suggesting that an individual needs to feel good about himself in order to be responsible and accountable for his actions even if the actions are contrary to the laws and include breaking the laws. Performance and conforming to rules and societal norms become secondary to the individual's need to feel good and have a position in society. The thinking continues that the criminal, who did not accept and learn from the available education, is then unable to secure a decent job and turns to crime to support his lifestyle. The philosophy is not that the individual fails and is held accountable, but that the system fails and is responsible.

If individuals failed to learn or could not be taught the accepted patterns of lawful behavior, minimal education standards, and job preparation skills outside the prison; how then, can we assume that all these skills will be taught and learned within the confines of the prison? We cannot, of course. However; our prisons are mandated to offer extensive education classes where prisoners can earn a high school diploma. Some prisons provide education beyond high school. Many prisoners have obtained college degrees while in prison. Do any prisons give classes in obeying the law, character development, moral codes of conduct, responsible behavior, and the difference between right and wrong — it appears that they do not teach these subjects because the rate of recidivism is rising.

Rehabilitation within the prison walls concerns itself with education, with physical conditioning, athletics, movies, television, and most of the conveniences enjoyed outside the prison. Through the rehabilitative efforts to make the prison look or feel as much like the outside community as possible, a wide variety of negative services and commodities have become available inside the prison. These services include the "prison hustle" where certain thugs can provide almost any service to other inmates for a fee. In *The Big House,* inmate Tom Lesce reveals the concept of this operation. This hustle is well-organized and is controlled like a business on the outside. The inside enterprise offers the sale of clothing, jewelry, sex, drugs, and weapons along with very stringent rules that the inmates must obey. Disobedience earns quick punishment, something the prisoners can easily understand. This prison hustle truly is one form of rehabilitation that benefits only certain inmates. This type of rehabilitation is on the wrong course.

Confession of a crime is the first step back in the rehabilitation process. When a person admits guilt for a wrongful deed he is giving voice to his conscience. The criminal is admitting that he has done something wrong. This admission of a crime is the essential moment when a criminal admits responsibility for his actions.

The courts, all the way up through the Supreme Court, push the Miranda Rights to its extreme. They prevent the acceptance of almost any confession being heard by a jury. Confessions that are purely voluntary may not be allowed if there is the slightest possibility of self-incrimination. And yet, that is what a large percentage of criminals want—self-incrimination—so they can admit their guilt. They want to pay for their crime and be punished so they can rejoin their family and the community. The confession of the criminal is the same as the child saying "Daddy (or Mommy), I'm sorry for what I've done, please forgive me and accept me back into the family."

The courts, by preventing confessions, are thwarting the true rehabilitation process. They are making a game out of the justice system and are themselves responsible for the breakdown of law and order in this country. By their efforts to insure prisoners' rights and prevent self-incrimination, the courts are frustrating the efficient, humane, and constitutionally approved methods of law enforcement. When a criminal cries out for help by confessing his crime he should be assisted on his way to recovery. He should not be stymied by some over-ly technical decision by a Supreme Court justice. The courts should not prevent this first, and most important, step on the road to rehabilitation.

Mandatory classes of instruction in moral values, positive behavioral changes, and civil obedience need to become part of the rehabilitation program. Classes in negative behavior modification and how to outwit the legal system seem to be taught. Most prison facilities maintain active law libraries and if an inmate learns anything it is how to challenge and appeal his conviction. Remorse for a crime committed is somehow not included in the vocabulary of prisoner rehabilitation or stressed by the ideologues of the rehabilitative agenda. Their interpretation of the problem is somewhat distorted and must be reviewed and changed.

Nowhere in the rehabilitation program is there concern for the crime victim. It appears that the compassion, the remorse, the *mea culpas,* and "I'm sorrys" were all acted out in the court-room during the trial for the benefit of the judge and jury. The victims of crime are punished or victimized twice. Once by the criminal who did them wrong, and again by a system that forces the victims—taxpayers—to pay for the rehabilitation of the criminals who wronged them! Truly something is wrong with a system that would wrong the victim of crime in an ef-fort to rehabilitate so very few criminals.

Perhaps we need a turn-around. Victims of crimes should apologize to their attackers for creating situations the criminals could not deal with, thus making them resort to their gangster ways. This attitude is consistent with the turn-the-other-cheek philosophy. It does; however, nothing to reduce the level of violence or frequency of crime. Cowering in the face of an attacker does not lessen the resolve of the attacker. If anything, weakness and acquiescence, emboldens the attacker since he does not fear counterattack or retribution. Vulnerability whets the appetite of the criminal and encourages more crime.

Not only are law-abiding citizens held responsible for crimes and criminals, but they are being held hostage and forced to act in certain ways by these criminals. The Los Angeles riots of the 1990s are an example of a country held hostage. First, a second trial was held to convict the police officers involved in the Rodney King beating despite the fact that a previous trial had been held concerning his arrest and beating. Double jeopardy was conveniently sidestepped so that a "proper outcome" could be obtained. Second, the people of Los Angeles were blatantly told that if the white police officers were not convicted there would be another riot! The people of L.A. were threatened by a riot if they did not act accordingly—convict the white officers. This same threat of criminal activity is used to rationalize and endorse holding law-abiding, taxpaying individuals hostage and threatening them with increased criminal activity if they do not support the present rehabilitation programs and pay for them. This is blackmail. Something is wrong with this system. There has to be a different approach with these criminals.

Rehabilitation programs are very expensive and only seem to punish the taxpayers who fund the programs. To the liberals, if only one thug or sociopath is rehabilitated then the rehabilitation movement justifies these programs no matter what the cost. All evidence indicates that almost no correcting or rehabilitating takes place in our present facilities. However, authorities of the rehabilitative effort argue to uphold the present programs despite their failure. We need to change our perspective of rehabilitating criminals now.

The Goals of a Correctional Program should be to:

1. Protect law-abiding citizens and their communities from the ravages of criminals and felons.

2. Reward law-abiding citizens by protecting and securing their rights over and above the rights of the criminals.

3. Insure that taxpayer dollars are spent wisely.

4. Evaluate the present correctional systems and determine which philosophies work and which systems waste taxpayer's money.

5. Weed out the nonproductive correctional systems and replace them with methods that work.

6. Learn from mistakes and correct them.

7. Rehabilitate criminals and return reformed, law-abiding offenders to our communities.

8. Accommodate all prisoners needing incarceration.

9. Keep all prisoners for the full term of their sentence.

10. Protect, feed, and house all prisoners within the system.

Chapter Five

Why Rehabilitation Does Not Work

Why Rehabilitation Fails

For the past one hundred years, the United States correctional system has been dominated by the rehabilitation philosophy. Reform, retrain, and rehabilitate have been the motto of our penal system. Correctional facilities have changed from places of punishment and confinement to gymnasiums and alternate schools. Every possible convenience and "prisoner right" has been granted in the hopes of rehabilitating the criminals.

Billions of dollars have been spent for prison construction to house our criminals more comfortably. Enormous sums of money have been spent on therapy and the education of criminals. Whenever an unmet need of prisoners was discovered, money was appropriated and efforts were made to satisfy the problem. Ironically, it seems the more money and compassion we lavish upon the correctional problem the less we realize in terms of true rehabilitation.

The American penal philosophy and thinkers have had one hundred years to test the efforts of rehabilitation as practiced today in our correctional institutions. Prison records and government data compiled over the decades have shown dismal results.

The landmark work by the late Robert Martinson, *What Works?—Questions and Answers about Prison Reform,* considered 231 studies that evaluated prisoner-offender treatment methods. Each study that was considered, had a control group to compare nontreated groups with treated groups. The results of Martinson's work showed that the rate of recidivism was not improved by treatment. It made no difference what kind of treatment was used for rehabilitation—nothing seemed to work. These studies have been reviewed by Walter C. Bailey and R. G. Hood. They support the findings that no method of treatment is effective in reducing the return to crime.

Essentially, Martinson's studies conclude that, in the manner of our current rehabilitation system, nothing works to reduce recidivism. It appears that the inability of rehabilitation is the total absence of punishment. The time-tested equation of rewards and punishment as educational factors is missing. The rewards side of the equation, represented by rehabilitation, community programs, education, and treatment are not balanced by any form of punishment. Being clothed, fed, and housed with your peers is a far cry from punishment. Here again, the hot stove analogy is appropriate. The burn—punishment—received by touching a hot stove is an adequate deterrent to stop a person from touching hot stoves.

To be an effective deterrent, any punishment must be swift and certain. Our judicial system frustrates the deterrence of possible punishment by long, drawn-out trials, mistrials for technicalities, plea bargaining, and the appeal process. Reuben Greenberg, Chief of Police in Charleston, S.C., promotes the thought of punishment as a deterrent to crime. In his book, *Let's Take Back Our Streets*, he cites an example of punishment—or the thought of punishment—as a deterrent to criminal action: A frail, little, 70-year-old, hunched lady who carried a shopping bag full of money through the most crime-infested section of New York City. The criminals all watched her pass by, knowing she carried large sums of money. She was a bag lady, a courier, for the numbers racket. She was unprotected; yet, nobody touched her. Everyone knew if they robbed her, their punishment would be quick, drastic, and final. Nobody touched the bag lady. It is too bad that our criminal justice system could not put the same fear of punishment into criminals to help protect American citizens.

Chief Greenberg echoes what Martinson and ex-governor of Colorado, Richard Lamm, said about the failure of our penal systems to rehabilitate: No form of therapy or rehabilitation program works to reduce recidivism. However, at about the age 35 to 40, the number of felons and ex-convicts, who are arrested again and sentenced to additional prison time, falls nearly to zero. It appears that the aging of the criminal is the only method that consistently works to reduce recidivism. Locking criminals up for prolonged time would allow them to age and lower their drive to act criminally. An added benefit of the prolonged incarceration or warehousing of criminals is their inability to commit crimes on our streets while they are behind bars.

Why have we failed in our efforts to rehabilitate criminals? Why have the billions upon billions of dollars and the devotion of countless correctional professionals failed to reform, let alone reduce, our criminal class? Are our efforts of dealing with criminals producing a less violent ex-convict? Has job training, psychological counseling, normalizing prison conditions, and insuring prisoners rights helped rehabilitate prisoners so that we live in a safer society? Has the emphasis on improving the social environment by enacting the Civil Rights Act, helping children with AFDC, housing allowances, medical coverage and all the numerous entitlement programs reduced our crime burden? No! A definite No! In fact crime has shown a parallel increase with the increase of entitlements.

Could it be that our compassionate efforts and dreams for rehabilitating criminals was doomed from the very beginning? Doomed because of false premises and not for lack of caring. We knew from the very outset that people could be trained and retrained. We knew that behavior modification could help change noncriminal behavior. We knew that immediate approval or punishment is the way behavior has been changed, or improved, since time immemorial. We also knew after decades of failures, as reported in our crime statistics, that behavior modification, as practiced in our current correctional facilities, did not seem to change criminals and their desire to lead a life of crime.

After decades of trying to change the criminals' behavior and reduce violence and crime we are forced to admit defeat.

We realize now that no matter how hard we have tried, our results from rehabilitation have been a total failure. We can not say we did not try. We may have tried too hard. Blinded as we were in our hopes of salvaging people who took the wrong road—the criminals—we concentrated on the symptoms of the crime. We need to admit that we did not quite understand the players involved. We were trying to deal with criminals as if they were regular, noncriminal, law-abiding people. We did not understand the workings of the criminal mind. We tried to use our knowledge and experience of how law-abiding people think and behave. We tried to extrapolate from what we knew of civil behavior and apply it to the criminal personality. At any rate—we were doomed to failure from the beginning.

In their exhaustive studies of the criminal mind and criminal personality which spanned 16 years, Dr. Yochelson and Dr. Samenow, concluded that criminals think differently than law-abiding people. As much as we would like to believe otherwise, criminals think and behave according to criminal thinking patterns. The main reason our rehabilitative efforts have failed is because we are using methods and techniques that work with noncriminals. These accepted methods do not work with criminals. One could say—"we are dealing with a different breed of cat".

Criminals are different from noncriminals. They think differently and behave differently. They do not learn to live by the standard values and teachings or react the same way as noncriminals do. From an early age, criminals develop patterns of behavior and ways of thinking that manipulate and exploit their families and friends, their communities, and the law-abiding society.

In our hope to rehabilitate and reform the criminal, we used methods which we knew worked with normal, noncriminal people. We were dismayed when our efforts failed and so we tried harder. When we experienced continued failure, we lamented that we did not do enough—we should have done more.

It is not politically correct to think that some people, the criminals, may be different from the rest of us. These people take what they want, they live by the law of the jungle. They exploit every situation to their advantage without any concern for other individuals. If, or when, they appear to be conforming to societies' rules, they do so as a cover to hide their criminal activities. They are bored with the norm of society and need to control others and follow through with their distorted thought patterns. To accept that some people, from early in life, are mean, cruel, vicious, exploitive, and manipulative conjures up thoughts of the "bad seed". This thought has been in disfavor because it touches a raw nerve that there may be a genetic basis for crime.

We know that some animals are mean and vicious. We have enacted laws to control pit bulldogs. Pit bulldogs are known to be mean and will attack people as well as other dogs. The smart person learns not to trust a Pit bulldog. Likewise, German Shepard dogs are implicated in 90% of dog bite victims seen in emergency rooms. It is prudent to give Pit bulls and German Shepards a wide berth. Golden Retrievers, on the other hand, almost never bite people. One can trust Golden

Retrievers. There is a distinct difference in certain animals; some are vicious, some are kind, some are trustworthy and some are not. So it is with the human animal. Most are trustworthy, kind, and compassionate—these are the law-abiding, hard working people that give stability to our codes of behavior and reinforce civil behavior. Others are cruel, conning, and manipulative—these are the criminals who have destroyed our sense of security and now control how we go about life.

The criminal personality starts out early in life by conning and manipulating parents and siblings. This is done through charm and intimidation or outright disobedience. He learns to control classmates and teachers for his own personal gain. Later in life he deviously manages employers and co-workers with lying and stealing on the side. Criminals also control wives and husbands to their own advantage. This manipulation continues throughout life with friends, family, and society.

When caught and convicted, the criminal shrewdly manipulates the legal system and the psychotherapists. These lawbreakers blame their behavior on others claiming that they have been mistreated, abused, not loved enough, and that they are disadvantaged. They reason that without these external forces they would behave like most citizens, but,since they were "victimized", they had no other recourse than to become a criminal. They are smart and have conned us all. We have succumbed to their faulty rationale and have pushed the criminal agenda of being a "victim" to the ridiculous. We have realized a sky-rocketing increase of criminal activity because we are naive and did not realize we were being manipulated.

In efforts to reclaim our prodigal sons—the criminals—the correctional psychiatrists and criminologists who are intent on curing the disease of crime, overlook the criminal way of thinking and acting. They try to excuse criminal behavior by looking to external factors, or "root causes" to explain the criminals' behavior. They try to separate the person from the crime. They have convinced themselves that the criminal is an ordinary person who became infected with the virus of crime. They now can concentrate their efforts toward curing the criminal's disease. This gives credence for attacking the root causes of crime which include poor education, poverty, broken families, poor job training, run-down neighborhoods, ethnic affiliation, racial status, and whatever other cause one can imagine.

Unfortunately, extensive probing and research has failed to prove that these root causes actually cause crime. Each possible cause does not stand up when subjected to unbiased examination. Poverty, for example, has been touted as a "root cause" of crime. But when it is shown that many people living in poverty are not criminals, the argument fails to support it as a probable cause. When it is shown that current neighborhoods that are less poverty-stricken than they were in the past, have higher crime rates now, the argument fails again. When it can be shown that the welfare entitlements have reduced the hardship of poverty, but have seemingly fostered a rise in crime, the argument for poverty as a root cause of crime is weakened further. And again the question may be asked, "Did a poor neighborhood cause the crime or is the neighborhood poor because of crime?"

And so it is with all the touted root causes: There is no external cause of crime. Criminal thought and behavior is not caused by any external force. The criminal thought comes from within the person who leads the life of a criminal. The criminal knows right from wrong. He has a chance to behave. However, he finds it more exciting to do things his way than to behave and follow the boring crowd. The criminals' motto is "Beaten paths are for beaten men". The criminal does what he wants to do when he wants to do it. He will bide his time by acting like a law-abiding person until the time is right for him to strike out. If he wants to behave according to civil rules to gain some advantage, he will; but, he will misbehave when it suits his fancy. The criminal is an expert at conning people for his benefit. He sees nothing wrong with his actions and actually believes he is a good person. He may act sorry and remorseful if it furthers his cause, but the true criminal is not sorry for anything he has done; he is only sorry that he messed up and was caught.

Our present system is totally unprepared and unable to cope with the criminals' mindset and the criminal personality. Any acquiescence by the system to prisoner demands and desires, will be considered a weakness and will be exploited to the full extent by the prisoner. Whenever the system gives in to the criminal, the criminal has won. This is commonplace today as we read about prisoners suing because they have no televisions or other amenities. In our efforts to be humane and to make sure we do not inflict "cruel and unusual punishment", the correctional system has become the victim of criminal exploitation. The prisoner uses and exploits every situation and every person to serve his purposes. The prisoners are winning, not the system that is supposed to rehabilitate them and change their behaviors.

The search for root causes has had its effects. Those who subscribe to this doctrine can push agendas to correct these causal factors of crime. This is the same agenda that ushered in the entire welfare-entitlement program that was going to cure poverty and crime. Those who championed the root cause philosophy can make themselves feel good because they believe they are treating causes—almost like treating a disease.

In medicine, we try to cure disease. Our efforts are aimed at eliminating or removing the infectious agents from the patient. Antibiotics are prescribed to kill the bacteria—a root cause of a patients' illness. Chemotherapy and x-rays are used to kill malignant cells—a root cause of the patients' cancer. Sometimes we resort to surgery to cut out the tumor—the root cause that is preying upon the patient.

The difference between a sick patient and a criminal is that patients seek out medical care because they do not feel well. They know something is wrong with them and they want to be cured. A prisoner, on the other hand, does not volunteer to go to prison to be cured for a sickness he does not feel he has. Why? Because he does not feel ill or think he is sick. He does not want or need to be cured. As long as he does not run afoul of the law and get caught, he is perfectly happy with his life. However, the criminologists believe the prisoner is a sick patient in need of treatment. Until they change their mindset, our present rehabilitation efforts will continue to fail. We must recognize that the criminal himself, is the disease that needs cured.

The other effect of root causes is that it gives the criminal some justification for his criminal activities. The authorities rationalize…'even though he committed a crime, he wouldn't have done it if he wasn't forced to by falling victim to some root cause'. This same justification for criminal activity can embolden people with noncriminal minds to commit crimes. They feel they are victims of some root cause that is society's fault. Take racism as an example. When people are constantly told they are victims of racism they will want to fight back. They will feel justified, as in the south central Los Angeles riots, to terrorize, loot, kill, and pillage.

When government agencies and political agendas support and promote these root causes and victimization, it removes the stigma of criminal behavior by embracing the notion that the criminals are victims of society, therefore they are allowed to fight back. This search for and interest in the root causes of crime, shifts the emphasis away from the criminal and focuses attention on external factors. Factors that do not stand scientific investigation to be the true causes of crime.

The rehabilitative movement has been caught up too long by the root causes of crime that they created and nurtured over the years. Rehabilitation has failed with criminals because the movement has failed to accept the following facts:

1. the criminal is responsible for his crimes;

2. the criminal must be held personally responsible for the crimes he has committed;

3. criminals, not law-abiding societies, cause crimes;

4. criminals seek out crime wherever they can find it;

5. criminals are a breed apart;

6. the criminal mind and the criminal personality resists any attempt at change; and

7. the criminal mind will exploit the prison situation just as surely as it manipulated society and the judicial system outside the prison.

When incarcerated, the criminal will exploit the correctional system. He will act remorseful and pretend to be sorry for what he has done. He will confess to having found religion and will no longer be a criminal. This short-lived act will gain him favor with guards and the parole board. It might shorten his time behind bars. However, once the prisoner is released, he returns to and continues his old ways of thinking and acting. Some are smart enough to lay low for awhile. Others are not.

Prisoners are masters at conning prison social workers and psychologists. The prisoner's act of sudden revelation and repentance for crimes committed after a counseling session bolsters the psychologists' ego and makes him feel like the prisoner is gaining insight into his behavior. The psychologist leaves the session feeling good about himself—the prisoner is laughing because he has conned "the shrink". After a few rap sessions with the therapist, a prisoner can substantiate his victim status on a more intellectual basis. The prisoner has also learned how to use psychology for excuses to be used in future crimes.

The current rehabilitation philosophy stresses freedom for prisoners. The inconvenience of incarceration is viewed as too stressful for convicts who have been victimized all of their lives by the pressures of a strict and demanding society. Life inside the prison is scheduled to alleviate the stress of confinement and boredom by providing day rooms with television, voluntary education classes, exercise yards, and whatever recreational outlets are needed to help keep peace in the prison.

Our current form of rehabilitation fails to consider the criminal personality with relation to the various recreational and stress programs. These very programs that were designed to benefit prisoners by eliminating boredom and frustration have become fertile breeding grounds for prisoner unrest. Convicts have exploited and manipulated the exercise and recreational periods to their own benefit. Prison gang violence, assaults, murders, rapes, and riots can be planned during these lapses in prisoner control. When the prison gang becomes a mob within the day room or the exercise yard nobody is safe. The authority of the guards is no longer present—the convicts rule. The criminal mentality has won again.

Allowing groups of criminals to intermingle for recreation goes counter to any real goal of rehabilitation. Criminals do not spend their recreational times together discussing how they are becoming more law-abiding and lamenting the damage they have done. When criminal minds unite they talk about excitement. They talk about how they can plan and exploit their present situation to their benefit. They talk about the mistakes they made that led to their arrest and conviction. They discuss ways to prevent future conviction after they are released and return to their chosen profession of crime. The current philosophies of rehabilitation are not only failing to reform—they are helping to make smarter criminals by promoting the free flow of criminal thought during stress management sessions in the yard, the exercise room and elsewhere throughout the prison.

Job training and education while in prison has always appealed to the correctional community. Prisoners are allowed out of their cells to participate in activities that are designed to alleviate, or at least correct, a few of the root causes—poor job training and education—of criminal behavior. Attendance at job training and educational classes allow prisoners some freedom. Freedom to interact and behave on a more normal level. Freedom to act and learn just like people on the outside. It was believed that this experience would translate into more civil law-abiding behavior when the prisoner was released back into society. Such is not the case.

Many times the job skills learned in prison are not compatible with the up-to-date job techniques in the marketplace. More importantly, the prisoner doesn't want a job in the first place. He would rather lead an exciting life of crime. Job training was fine while in prison to break the boredom of incarceration, but a lifetime of drudgery, working at a dull, low-paying job is not appealing. If the prisoner wanted to work, he would have learned and used the job skills on the outside before he came to prison.

The same goes for education. Prisoners found schools boring and uninteresting. Sitting in a classroom with a bunch of "nerds" obeying silly rules is not very exciting. Prisoners chose to drop out of school and lead more exciting lives. Those prisoners who did stay in school, for whatever reason, do not need classroom instruction in prison. They may attend class to help fill out an unexciting prison routine. Most prisoners are not learning per se. They attend classes to make a good impression on their counselors, instructors, and the parole board. Some prisoners take advantage of legal education to pursue their appeal process and thereby shorten their time behind bars. In any case, the job and educational programs offered in prison do not express themselves by lower rates of recidivism or lower crime rates upon prisoner release. Very little actual long-term rehabilitation has taken place. The prisoners are; however, happy to use the system while incarcerated if for no other reason than to break the monotony of prison life. We must not be fooled into thinking that these programs are rehabilitating anybody.

Figures revealing the high rate of recidivism tell a sad story. The story that is not told may be worse. No one knows the percentage of criminals that are released back into society that continue lives of crime. Criminals that have learned how to follow lives of crime without getting caught. Criminals who have learned the various techniques to beat-the-system and still make a living from crime. Criminals who have learned that crime pays—as long as you are careful and do not mess up.

We must realize that until we change our current rehabilitation philosophy, we are actually aiding and abetting crime on our streets. This is done by letting the criminals and would-be offenders know that life in the prison is not too bad. It is done by reducing whatever deterrent effect prison may have in reducing crime. Every study indicates the failure of our current methods of reformation. The failure is a direct result of not knowing with whom we are dealing, along with a failure to realize and understand how criminals think and act.

We must focus on the criminal, not society, the environment, root causes, or any number of unproven causes of criminal behavior. We must realize that crime comes from the individual criminal. Crime is something the criminal chooses to do. Criminal activity is a well thought out plan of behavior. Crimes of passion, like almost all forms of criminal activity, have behavior patterns leading up to the crime expression. Criminals are responsible for crimes. Criminals think differently about rules and regulations, they think differently about truth and loyalty.

According to Reuben Greenberg, a criminal evaluates the risks of crime. He says the criminal balances the risks against the benefits and rewards of his criminal behavior. The criminal then opts to commit a crime because it is quicker, easier, and the most cost-effective way of reaching his goals. Chief Greenberg states that criminals know the rules of civil and decent behavior—they just do not abide by them. They can not defer gratification—they take what they want when they want it.

We can only make our crime situation worse by allowing the criminal to use the excuse that he was a victim and was forced to behave in a criminal way. Everyone in the correctional and judicial system must insure that the criminal be held accountable for his crimes. We will only rehabilitate when we enforce a system of rewards and punishment that the criminal mind can understand.

Chapter Six

Cost of Security and Corrections
The High Price of Security and Incarceration

When a person thinks of prisons, one visualizes large, gray buildings surrounded by walls and security fences. We sometimes fail to consider prisons as an integral and inseparable part of a large and very expansive system: a complex that encompasses the multifarious facets of our total police and security networks; a network that extends from the top levels of our federal police and security forces down through our local police and sheriff departments. It is easy to overlook the fact that the prisons and their costs are a significant part of our overall security and protection system.

Our correctional facilities include the various levels of prisons, jails, community half-way houses, and all the many forms of incarceration and correction. It encompasses the many non-incarceration aspects of correction such as probation and parole. It also includes the various forms of retraining camps and community outreach programs. Truly, our prisons represent a very interconnected and expensive part of our everyday lives. Our tax dollars pay for a monolithic structure.

Our current expenditure for prisons and the confinement of prisoners is staggering and continues to take larger and larger amounts of taxpayer's money. According to figures compiled by John J. DiIulio, Jr., in his book *No Escape*, Americans spent an estimated $20 billion on incarcerated, convicted criminals in 1988. These are the estimated direct costs of incarceration. Other sources estimated higher spending for incarceration. Now, in 2005, the costs have possibly doubled.

These costs are escalating. Between fiscal year 1987 and fiscal year 1988, correction spending increased by 10% nation-wide. This trend is continuing and there is no letup in sight. In fact, present overcrowding, and the increase in crime rates are pushing the future costs and projected spendings higher and higher. Recent legislative proposals for more police and more prisons will increase our security costs.

We are faced with a more costly correction-rehabilitation system just to satisfy our current confinement needs. Taxpayers and local communities are demanding that the lawless be locked up and taken off the streets in order to reduce the crime in our neighborhoods. They are also suggesting that violent juvenile offenders be handled and incarcerated as adults to remove them from streets.

Taxpayers are becoming restive and are tired of paying for a system that does not produce good results; measured by the rate of recidivism and the failure to reduce our escalating crime rates. We need to use the system properly to get the desired results. Present needs, plus projected future demands to keep pace with the increasing crime statistics, predict that the costs of incarceration will increase remarkably.

In spite of the fact that our prison and correction system is enormously expensive, it is cost-effective if used properly. Cost-effective, by simply incarcerating and removing the criminal from the community, thereby preventing more crimes. The economist Edwin Zedlewski analyzed the cost-benefit ratio of incarceration. He found that, in the 1980s and early 1990s, the average cost of confining a career criminal in prison was about $25,000 per year. Other researchers have estimated the confinement rates per year to be much higher. As stated previously, these rates may have already doubled.

A study published by the National Institute of Justice, which used data from the 1980s and early 1990s, worked with the figure of $25,000 per year for prisoner confinement, and found it to be cost-effective when compared with the alternative of allowing career criminals to go free. The study reasoned that career criminals commit between 187 and 287 crimes per year. When all the direct costs, such as criminal justice, victim losses, and prosecution are added to the indirect costs, such as home, auto, and private security systems one arrives at a rough figure of $2,300 per crime. Multiplying the conservative figure of 187 crimes per year by the cost of $2,300 per crime gives a total of $430,100 cost to society for each criminal not incarcerated and confined. Subtracting $25,000 from $430,100 means a savings to society of $405,100 per year for each criminal incarcerated.

What Do We Pay for Our Security?

It is difficult to determine the direct costs of our security. It is next to impossible to separate the direct costs from the indirect costs and arrive at some figure that comes close to our security and crime-fighting expenses. Direct and indirect costs are interrelated and merge into one another clouding cost estimates. We are left with vague estimates. We know that our security service costs are enormous and touch our daily lives directly and indirectly. Directly by our victimization and indirectly through the many costs that crime places on our society.

Let us examine the facets of our security system to see if we can gain insight as to how our security dollars are being spent. Corrections spending includes not only the cost of prison construction and maintenance, but all the related security and protection services that support the prison facility. These support services include, but are not limited to, the various police forces from our federal crime-fighting agencies—FBI, ATF, DEA, etc.—down through our state highway patrol and local enforcement officers and the many private security companies.

Additionally, our security outlay supports the entire judicial system which includes judges, bailiffs, numerous office staffs, trial lawyers, district attorneys, court recorders, law clerks, and all the other ancillary staff. It encompasses all the personnel in the prisons and the community-based and supported facilities. It includes all the support staff that keeps our prisons running such as maintenance, transportation, medical personnel, and rehabilitation workers. The outlay embodies all the correction officers outside the prison walls such as social workers, probation and parole officers, and many other welfare and prison support service workers.

And finally, the correction system must pay the expense of housing, feeding, retraining and rehabilitating the inmates. The prisoners must be given medical and dental care and their families supported by welfare, food stamps, housing allowance, aid to dependent children, and all the entitlement programs that have fostered and supported the American underclass which is linked to the crime explosion. Often times, prisoners continue receiving unemployment checks while incarcerated. Truly, the tentacles of prison costs are far-reaching and are woven into the very fabric of our society.

Additional Costs

Many factors determine just how our security dollars are spent on the state, county, and local levels. Demands for protection and security drive the expenditures, and the demand is generated by need. We need more security in our high-density urban centers because there is more crime in these areas. Therefore, more state moneys will be used to fight crime in the urban areas.

The tax base and the wealth of a given city or state may be determining factors in the moneys allocated for security. Luckily, some of the poorer states have largely agricultural assets, small farming communities, and few large crime-infested cities. These agricultural areas, with their belief in moral, religious and family values, do not generate the amount of crime that one finds in the large cities. The state of Kansas, for instance, registers more crime in Wichita, Kansas City, and

Topeka, than in the remainder of the state. This picture is duplicated in many other states. The rural, less densely populated areas, have less crime than the suburban and urban areas. It follows that the preponderance of security dollars are spent fighting crime in the urban population centers.

The crime-fighting efforts in our cities throughout the nation affects many facets of community life. Large and small businesses, along with schools, churches, and private homeowners are taking precautionary measures to insure the safety of their neighborhoods. In hopes of preventing and fighting crime, many individuals invest in extra locks on their homes and vehicles. Some purchase watchdogs and install extra lighting in their homes and yards to ward off potential thieves and vandals. Others use sophisticated security systems for their homes and vehicles and subscribe to neighborhood security patrols by private companies. These all figure into the direct and indirect costs of crime and security and it is next-to-impossible to separate these expenditures.

The costs of crime are far-reaching and affect us all. Whereas, the victim of a criminal act may be able to assess direct physical and property damage in dollars, the indirect costs are difficult to ascertain. Besides the outlay for crime-fighting measures, we must also pay for crimes with immeasurable human suffering. There is no price for that loss. The victim of a vicious, violent crime with physical injuries must face hospital expenses, possible surgery, rehabilitation, and perhaps long-term psychological treatment. The medical, retraining, and rehabilitation costs are enormous and difficult to measure. Injured victims will probably be unable to work. The victim may lose a job. Funeral expenses are another cost of crime that the victims bear. Truly, we live in a crime-infested country and our entire lives are impacted, directly and indirectly, in combating crime.

It is difficult to separate the expenses of confining felons from the routine police service of traffic control, crowd management, and citizen assistance. The costs are all intertwined. Needless to say, every citizen-taxpayer has a vested interest in our security and correctional systems.

Prisoner detention runs the gamut from maximum security facilities down through minimum security residences, half-way houses, and the various types of community-based facilities. John J. DiIulio, Jr., reports that in 1989, some 3.6 million Americans were under some form of correctional supervision or incarceration in the United States. He listed 675,000 people in prisons, over 300,000 in jails, and the remainder, which is the majority and three-fourths of the convicted population, to be in various community-controlled probation, retraining facilities, and parole programs. More recent figures from the U.S. Department of Justice, in 1991, lists 792,000 people in prisons and 424,000 in jails. This constitutes an enormous number of individuals to care for, house, and feed. The 2004 figures of the number of prisoners would more than likely be double what the 1991 figures showed, and the overall costs would have doubled. Department of Justice figures show an increase in the overall number of people in the correctional system. And it follows that the overall costs continue to rise.

Other sources have tried to estimate the costs of incarceration by averaging the cost per inmate per year. These expenses vary depending on the security level of the facility, the geographic location, and the size of the institution. Once again we get caught in the quagmire of direct and indirect costs of these outlays. Figures vary from $10,000 per inmate per year in some southern states to amounts close to $55,000 per inmate per year in other states depending on security levels. It is difficult to know what these figures are measuring. Do these numbers include the simple price of housing, feeding, and staffing or do they take into account the overall expense of the police activities in the communities that apprehended these individuals? Does it include the judicial system, the numerous social agencies, the parole and probation departments, the cost of prison construction, and all the many associated agencies that support the correctional system? All one knows is that it is a staggering amount to pay for a system that admits its failure by the rising tide of crime, unsafe communities, and the high recidivism rates. This correctional system is big business and taxpayers foot the bill.

One would expect that for an average $25,000 to $ 55,000 per inmate per year we would get a well-behaved, rehabilitated member of society ready to assume his or her role in a peaceful community. On the contrary; we get a hardened, more violent thug who has obtained a masters degree in criminality and wants to "get even". We get an ex-con who thinks he can beat-the-system next time. Behind the prison walls each convict has an opportunity to hone his criminal skills and dream of how he can practice those skills on the streets of society.

The number of criminals is growing everyday and the problem of overcrowding demands that new incarceration facilities be built. Along with this demand is the increase in the cost of each inmate per year. When the cost of a prison is listed anywhere from $15 million per facility and on upwards to hundreds of millions of dollars, one can only wonder what we are paying for and what we will receive for that outlay. The end of the spiraling costs is nowhere in sight. Is there a better method? We need to reexamine our thinking.

Many states and cities have prison construction as a priority to relieve the present overflow of prisoners. Many critics say that besides the high price of prison construction, the immense staffing and management that seems to be necessary to handle our current prisons, is as much a problem as the overcrowding that is so prevalent in so many facilities today. Even if billions of dollars were used to build prisons, the staffing would be a limiting factor. Perhaps, now is the time to consider a new concept.

The Iso-Rehab concept, discussed herein, is a restructuring of our correctional system from the ground up. If building prisons is a means to control crime and deal with the present overcrowding, perhaps Iso-Rehab facilities should be considered. They are far less expensive to build, much safer for all who are incarcerated in them, and they create an ideal atmosphere for rehabilitation and learning. They take only a fraction of the staff to maintain. It is truly worth giving the Iso-Rhab an evaluation and a fair chance. We have to take control and change the present failing, expensive systems that have proven non effective over many decades. Let us consider Iso-Rehab.

Chapter Seven

Iso-Rehab Can Correct

Welcome to the World of Iso-Rehab

Throughout this book, references have been made to "Iso-Rehab" and how it is the answer to what ails our present correctional system. The term itself is short for Isolation-Rehabilitation which is a dual concept that employs isolation as a first step and principal factor in the rehabilitation process. It addresses many of the current problems and faults of the modern prison system. One may be wondering how it is used and why it will work and how it is different and better than the present methods? These and many other questions will be answered along with explanations of this methodology and why it can answer many of today's problems.

There are many benefits to this dual concept of isolation and rehabilitation. The basic method of isolating the inmate is the foundation upon which the program is built: *Remove the inmate from all sources of danger and distraction and make him comfortable.* This concept is surely ideal for every inmate, but some will not benefit from it with regard to the rehabilitation process. Those will remain in, or be transferred to, the present prison system.

A thorough screening of prospective inmates and their complete criminal history will be required before acceptance. If accepted, each inmate's history will be used to formulate a specific rehabilitation program. This personalized plan will depend mainly upon taped audio messages created specifically for each inmate.

Initially, these individualized recorded messages will be played overhead several times throughout the day. Messages will stress respect for law and order, moral values, codes of conduct, acceptable behavior, and other disciplines. As time progresses, the programs will be upgraded on an individual basis and geared toward molding acceptable, responsible behavior for the future. Stress will be placed on the misery and suffering the criminals' behavior has caused the family, the friends, the community and especially the victims of their crime. General education programs will be offered and encouraged. Various educational broadcasts will have varying levels of intensity which will augment the inmates' needs as he progresses in the system.

Inmates upon arrival, will be given, via messages from above — on the unit intercom—a complete set of rules and regulations that they must obey throughout their stay. Inmates will have limited rights while confined here as part of the rehabilitation process. They will be informed that their cell unit is their only environment for the length of their confinement. They will be informed of the consequences of misconduct while at this facility. There will be a schedule of daily activities offered to each inmate. There will be three nourishing meals a day, exercise time, shower time, and plenty of time to reflect about where and how they went wrong and why they must change. Being isolated from nearly everyone and everything, the inmates will soon learn the importance of following rules and regulations, responsibility for their surroundings, and accountability for their actions.

The whole period of incarceration in Iso-Rehab will be a beneficial learning process, relearning process if you will, that will teach each inmate to respect himself and others, follow codes of conduct, and the importance of becoming a productive, responsible member of society. Many will need an attitude change as well as behavior modifications. Inmates must realize that they are not the true victims as modern sympathies suggest. They are incarcerated because they have victimized someone. These criminals must realize that they can not disobey laws or hurt someone merely because they want to, and think they can get away with it. They must realize that they will be punished for any crime they commit. They must learn to respect life and the values that civilized citizens hold dear.

There are rules and regulations to life that prisoners have learned but have refused to follow. To function in society, these criminals must be made aware of these rules and abide by them always, not just when they want to. Discipline and obeying rules is important. The prisoners are incarcerated because they did not follow the rules. They must change the way they think and behave. This change in attitude, with emphasis on discipline, will help them return to society with a different outlook and become productive rather than return to crime. These changes will all be promoted with Isolation-Rehabilitation.

History of Isolation in American Prisons

Dwight C. Jarvis, in his book, *Institutional Treatment of the Offender*, states:

"Sir Walter Crofton developed the reformatory system in the mid-1800s and used three stages in his system: The first stage was the solitary confinement stage. Prisoners were isolated to think about their crimes.

The second stage of Crofton's reform allowed prisoners to live and work together on public projects such as road building. The third stage permitted the prisoners to work outside the prison without supervision. Any failure of the prisoners' behavior would return him to the stage he came from."

Historically, the Pennsylvania System—also known as the Pennsylvania Plan—used a model of solitary confinement that offered criminals time, peace, and quiet. Each prisoner had his own living cell and an exercise area. It was considered a humane form of incarceration as it provided peace, security, and time for thought. Several other states copied the Pennsylvania Plan; however, economic factors caused a shift to the New York-Auburn Plan of penal management. A plan that could use cheap inmate labor for prison industry. Many of our correctional facilities today were patterned after the Auburn Plan and still have prison industry as their main focus for prisoner control and rehabilitation.

It should be noted that the Pennsylvania Plan was considered very humane and was changed for economic reasons. The shortcoming of this plan was the lack of programmed instruction to reform the criminals and their behavior. The Iso-Rehab program adds personalized reform instruction to the solitary security of the Pennsylvania Plan. It does not take advantage of prisoners as a source of cheap labor and call it rehabilitation.

Isolation helps prevent the phenomenon of institutionalization from happening. Studies have shown that when prisoners adapt to the correctional institution; that is, when they become socialized to the prison environment, they become institutionalized. The more institutionalized a prisoner becomes, the more likely he will be to return to the prison environment upon being released. Studies have shown that the younger the prisoner is when incarcerated and the longer a convict stays in prison, the more likely he is to return to the prison upon release.

Isolation prevents the dehumanizing that occurs with prisoners as they accept the role of a prisoner and try to conform to the wishes of other prisoners. They lose their personal identity as they assume the prisoner role and become socialized as prisoners, often setting aside their personal feelings, beliefs, ideals, and values. The inmates lose their self-image as they strive to play their expected role. They lose self-identity and become dehumanized. The Iso-Rehab prevents this dehumanization. The Iso-Rehab inmate has no one to impress and no role to play.

Isolation

Whenever the term isolation is used in connection with our penal systems, the liberals among us start quaking with fear that we are returning to the dark ages. In fact, whenever any penal program attempts to alter a convict's life or environment, it is met with resistance and cries of prisoner cruelty.

The "enlightened" penal and correctional thinking implies that life behind bars should approach, as nearly as possible, life in the law-abiding community. This compassionate liberal thinking attempts to provide the amenities within the prison that normal citizens enjoy on the outside. The liberal-minded correctional thinkers have gone so far as to request and to provide color television sets in prisoner cells.

Making sure that prisoners have all their rights and can spend their time behind bars with a minimum of discomfort imposed on them from the authorities has been the correctional goal for several decades. Prisoners can leave their gang on the outside and join the prison gang behind the walls with little disruption in their daily routines. Many prisoners make new friends within the prisons and are often reunited with old buddies and gang members when they suffer the inconvenience of being incarcerated.

There are few restrictions that the prison environment imposes on prisoners. These include staying in your room at certain times, eating at specified times, showering with fellow convicts, not causing riots, and not assaulting or raping fellow inmates. Prisoners are still able to hang out with their gangs in the exercise yard, almost like hanging out on a street corner.

About the only enforceable restrictions that are imposed is the staying in your room at specified times—the lock up.

Any effort to modify a prisoners' lifestyle behind bars and to change the way prisoners think has been met with resistance from the courts, the liberals, and the prisoners themselves. The efforts to maintain the status quo have worked. Our present system maintains the convict life style and mindset. Prisoners don't want to be rehabilitated. In fact, it appears that prisoners have the right—protected by the courts—not to be reformed and rehabilitated. They have the "right" to be returned to society and get-on-with-their-lives after their time has been served.

Yes, the "enlightened" penal thinking we have endured for the past several decades has ensured that no real change can or has taken place with regards to reforming prisoner behavior. All of the innovative forms of correction have prevented, by this soft-headed compassion, any real reform or rehabilitation of prisoners. The majority of law-abiding citizens are demanding that something be done with a failing system. They are fed up with a system that does not work.

One might ask; Why can't we demand that true efforts at rehabilitation and reform be made since that is what we are paying for with our tax dollars? Only the courts and the liberal activists can answer that question.

The first step in correcting the current program demands a change of thinking. We need to take bold measures and change the way we think. We thought that by normalizing prison conditions and bending over backwards to make prison life comfortable we would rehabilitate the prisoners. We were wrong. As with any entitlement program, the more we give the more they take.

Prisoners have proven by their crimes and their behavior that their thinking and their behavior is faulty—a court of law has deemed their actions and their thought patterns to be not only flawed, but criminal. Prisoners have, it can be argued, lost the right to continue their criminal thinking and behavior. It can also be argued that until they are rehabilitated they must surrender some rights.

Today, prisoners do not have to reform to regain their rights. In our current system, the prisoner has nothing to work for, nothing to gain—he already has his rights. The courts insure that prisoners have rights that are inviolate. Why should a prisoner reform?

It is time for the courts to help rehabilitate the correction system. They can do that by making a change in the pattern of behavior that fosters and nurtures crime. The courts must allow and encourage a philosophy that breaks the criminal behavior pattern. The first step in breaking the criminal mold is to remove the criminal from all the influences that caused the criminal behavior; that is, isolate the prisoner from his environment. A "get tough" stance would indicate the courts are serious about rehabilitating prisoners.

Only by separating a prisoner from the causes of crime—his environment, his reaction and his thinking about his environment—can we hope to change the patterns of behavior that led to criminal activity and crime. By removing ones finger from the hot stove, one prevents further pain and burning. So it is with crime and criminal behavior—isolate the criminal quickly before he becomes burned and scarred by the fires of the criminal environments.

The first step in healing the burned finger is removing it from the fire. Criminals deserve no less. Prisoners have the right to be removed from their crime-causing situations. They have the right to be isolated and to be reformed. They have the right to be retrained in their thought patterns so they can be returned to society as productive new people.

Prisoners may not know—shown by their records that they don't understand the implications of their behavior—that they need strict isolation to alter the pattern of their lives. Prisoners may resist any efforts to change their behavior. Small children resist their mother's efforts to make them take an afternoon nap even though the child is falling asleep and showing signs of fatigue. A mother's firmness will ensure that her child gets the nap he needs. Likewise, the prisoners' resistance must be met with firm resolve. They must be isolated as a first step in the healing process.

Amendment VIII of our *Bill of Rights* states: "Excessive bail shall not be required, nor excessive fines imposed, nor cruel and unusual punishments inflicted." In light of this amendment we can consider several questions regarding the constitutionality of the Iso-Rehab system.

Some people argue that isolation is cruel and unusual. They say that isolation would drive people insane. Let's examine the facts from the data that is available regarding isolation. History is replete with people who voluntarily opted for isolation for various reasons. Monks, gurus, priests, and scientists have, from time to time, chosen the privacy and serenity that solitude offered. Their isolation was, of course, voluntary. Isolation under such circumstances seems to do no harm to the isolated person even after prolonged exposure. What then, would be the results of forced or coerced isolation?

We have an extensive—clinical—trial that evaluates the effects of forced or involuntary isolation. Many of our prisoners of war were kept in forced isolation against their will. Moreover, many of the prisoners in such solitary confinement were ill-treated, abused, tortured, and sexually violated. These prisoners of war were not criminals and had committed no crimes against their fellow citizens which could have caused them to feel guilty and perhaps deserving of solitary confinement. Furthermore, many of our servicemen who were in solitary confinement experienced the worst of all possible conditions of darkness, damp and moldy surroundings, inadequate and unhealthy food, torture, and psychological trauma.

These veterans, upon being repatriated, attest to the durability and resiliency of the human spirit. Most kept the spirit of survival going in their minds by thinking of home, family, and the time-honored moral values. They did not have color televisions, radios, telephones, family visits, letters from home, nor any of the other amenities that today's prisoners enjoy routinely. Few ex-POWs show any mental problems directly associated with their isolation and being deprived of these modern conveniences. By and large these ex-POWs have returned to live normal lives.

Prisoners who misbehave may be put in the confines of solitary confinement—the hole. Studies have shown no deleterious, long-lasting effects from this confinement. Prison records show that solitary confinement has a salutary effect on the prisoners. It makes them all think twice before disobeying.

Isolation in the Iso-Rehab system, is a far cry from being uncomfortable. A clean, private room with toilet and bath facilities, and three meals a day is not uncomfortable. Isolation is a natural form of our daily lives. We are all essentially isolated from our surroundings when we sleep. If we sleep eight hours a day we are isolated for one-third of our lives. No one could argue that the isolation we experience during sleep is punishing or harmful. Confinement in Iso-Rehab completes the isolation circle and allows twenty-four hour control of the inmate. This control will eliminate outside distractions and counterproductive stimuli which would reduce the rehabilitative effort.

Isolation, to be effective within the Iso-Rehab system, means prisoners will have no outside contact. Isolation means isolation: secluded, cut off; segregated. To ensure a complete break with the pre-confinement environment; no personal effects, such as pictures, jewelry, or civilian clothes would be allowed. Clothing issued would consist of a light-weight shirt and a light-weight pair of boxer shorts or trousers. This type of clothing will be more than adequate and comfortable in the climate-controlled cells. Shoes, socks, and head coverings would be unnecessary. The garments would be picked up every third day and exchanged for a set of clean apparel .

Cutting off all ties with the outside world includes no television and no movies. Many authorities blame television and movies for fostering criminal behavior and isolation short-circuits this influence. No radio. Radio is banned because it would interfere with the programmed audio messages and rehabilitative instruction being sent to each prisoners' cell throughout the day. No telephones. Telephone contact is forbidden to prevent the inmate from conducting gang and criminal activity from within the prison. Barring telephones also halts drug deals and escape plans.

The families of the convicts may suffer slightly, but they too are part of the problem that fostered the criminals' behavior. They too need to reflect on what role they played as part of the problem. If, as the liberal philosophy states, the breakdown of families and the community is responsible for the environment that caused the criminal behavior in the first place, then it only makes sense to remove this bad influence from entering the prison via the telephone.

The prisoners will be allowed a twenty-minute family visit every three months. Two family members will be given the visit privilege; not more. Liberals may complain that restricting visits with family members is cruel and unusual. Let them consider the number of family visits our prisoners of war had during their captivity. Zero visits. These were not criminals. They were imprisoned while fighting for our freedom and way of life. Our government did not make much of a effort to free our G.I.s from their captivity and isolation. Therefore, our government should accept the isolation of prisoners to help in the rehabilitation process.

Psychological studies have shown that by removing all extraneous stimuli, test subjects are fixated upon the single stimulus they are receiving. So it will be with prisoners. Removal of all external stimuli will fix the convicts' full attention on the audio message presented as part of the rehabilitation curriculum.

Isolation will allow a continual programmed audio reeducation of the convict in an ideal learning environment. There will be no outside distractions. No worry of assault. No work. No drugs, alcohol or cigarettes. No worry or concern about where the next meal is coming from. No worry about being homeless. The only thing the prisoner will be concerned with is listening to and learning from the audio message and booklet (after two months in the Iso-Rehab unit, the prisoner will be given a booklet concerning moral values and laws) which accompanies the education programs.

By removing the prisoner from harmful influences, isolation prepares the inmate to accept helpful stimuli that can change harmful behavior patterns and lead to rehabilitation. Isolation in the Iso-Rehab system is not wasted or idle time. Isolation is used as a tool for correction. Isolation by itself has some rehabilitative value, but becomes more beneficial when combined with the proper educational programs. Isolation is time spent listening to programmed instruction and reflection upon the laws and moral values presented.

Isolating prisoners and removing all extraneous stimuli and influences prepares the prisoners to focus upon the stimuli that are introduced into each unit as part of the rehabilitation program. The importance of removing all outside distractions can not be stressed too much. It is important to have the prisoners' undivided attention so the rehabilitation message will have no interference. Any distraction will lessen the impact of the rehabilitation program and weaken the retraining efforts.

Isolation is similar to "cold turkey" which is probably the most effective way to quit the alcohol, tobacco, and drug habits. Abusers simply stop whatever dependency habit they have. They do not take small sips of alcohol, fewer cigarettes, or change a heroin habit for a methadone habit. They just stop the habit. The first few days may be rough, but if the commitment and desire to quit is strong enough they can succeed and beat the habit. Other methods of kicking the habit that rely on a step-down program and easing the shock of quitting, usually have a high percentage of failures and a high rate of recidivism. So it is with crime and criminal behavior. If a person is redeemable and able to be rehabilitated, going cold turkey and isolating oneself from all influences that supported and abetted the criminal behavior is the initial step on the road to recovery.

Saving the lives and futures of people that can be rehabilitated demands our best techniques which have proven successful: cold turkey, isolation, and discipline camps to name a few. It is time to stop coddling the abusers, the criminals, and the gangsters. They need to come face-to-face with their problems and cure themselves by stopping the behavior that leads to their afflictions, be it drugs, alcohol or criminal activity. Isolation gives them a chance to go cold turkey and separate themselves from the sources that helped lead them astray.

Benefits of Isolation

Isolating inmates from one another would prevent most of what is wrong with our current system. Prisoners in separate, clean, and escape-proof enclosures are safe from abuse by other inmates. A major concern of our prisons is protecting prisoners from physical abuse and trauma inflicted by other convicts. It is well-known that sexual abuse and sodomy is a constant threat within prisons. The threat of this attack is fearful enough; contracting AIDS from coerced and forced sodomy by other inmates is devastating. Intimidation, assault, and coercion to conform to the rules of the prison gang hierarchy is an expectation and standard behavior in our modern "enlightened" prison system.

Our prisons have confined or separated the criminals from society, but almost never separated inmates from one another. Rarely, if ever, is a prisoner isolated from the other prisoners as a means of protecting prison inmates. In our current prison system, isolation is used to control inmates who become unmanageable and become a problem with the orderly function of the prison. It is also used as punishment for prisoners who try to escape.

Judges, sentencing underage criminals, are often reluctant to place the youthful offenders in an adult facility for safety's sake. They are also hesitant to confine a "snitch" or a cop-gone-bad in a regular prison for fear that the person may not survive the prison justice handed down by other prisoners. Judges also discriminate in favor of white collar criminals. White collar criminals are almost never committed to regular state prisons. They are placed in federal facilities and minimal security institutions. Judges are aware of prison dangers and protect members of their own social class from these perils. This attests to the common knowledge that our prisons are not safe places.

As they are now managed, prisons are unsafe for the prisoners, the guards, and the community to which the ex-convicts return. About the only control the current prison system can exercise over the convicts is to house them. The prison warden can isolate the "bad prisoner" in a safe house within the prison for their misbehavior or in-house crimes. This practice is known as solitary confinement and is used as an extreme security measure. This trip to isolation allows the bad inmate to "cool off" before being reunited with the other prisoners. It also protects the other prisoners from a rogue. The isolation of rogues also adds to the tranquillity of the prison environment.

Judges, when handing down a sentence, may prescribe a number of years in prison with eligibility for parole and probation. They may sentence a criminal to be executed. Have you ever heard of a judge sentencing a person to a period of isolation? It would appear that judges prefer to have felons convicted of crimes, sent to unsafe, dangerous places for confinement. Places they know, by the record, do not rehabilitate or protect anyone. Places they know have been called "finishing schools" for criminals. Perhaps the ultimate joke or crime that American society plays on itself is the belief that our present prison system is humane and will help to cure the crime so rampant among us.

Isolating prisoners from each other prevents all the current abuses and alleviates the atmosphere of fright that prevents real rehabilitation from taking place. Isolating prisoners from one another would remove the hostile environment from the teaching program. Even the liberals would agree that it is next to impossible to learn in an unpleasant atmosphere and environment. How can they expect individuals who could not learn on the outside to suddenly learn and be rehabilitated on the inside with all the physical and psychological threats? Of course, one can not expect any rehabilitation under such adverse conditions. Is it any wonder our efforts to rehabilitate have failed?

Isolating inmates has numerous beneficial results:

1. protects prisoners from assault by other inmates;

2. prevents the transmission of AIDS via prisoner rape and homosexual activity;

3. reduces communicable diseases among the convicts;

4. halts criminal activity and further criminal education among prisoners;

5. allows prisoners time to think and learn without the threat of violence and intimidation;

6. allows convicts to reflect on their criminal behavior and the circumstances resulting from that behavior;

7. gives them time and privacy to repent for their crimes, if they are truly sorry for their misconduct.

Historically, many people and groups have chosen isolation for various reasons. Some scientists have removed themselves from society in order to think and ponder unsolved mysteries. Many men-of-God have taken vows of solitude to meditate and come closer to the truth. Monasteries, both in the Orient and the Occident, have devotees of isolation for purposes of revelation and reflection. Isolation has proven beneficial to many religious and righteous people and should; therefore, be no hardship on the tough individuals who become criminals. We know that criminals are tough survivors so we must assume that gangsters and thugs would thrive in a well-directed isolation program which was specially geared toward rehabilitation.

Political prisoners and prisoners of war have endured months and years of torture and isolation. Our government did little to rescue these prisoners. Our governments' failure to intervene can be interpreted as tacit approval that the enemy imprisons and detains our soldiers; many of them in isolation. All of the returning prisoners of war have attested, to a man, that the time they spent in isolation was given to pondering their situation and reflecting on their lives and futures. Not one of the POWs ever wanted to be in a position or situation where they could be returned to the stockade. These repatriated POWs have returned with an outlook that life is precious and make-the-most-of-it.

An extended time to ponder and reflect can be beneficial. The thought of sending convicted felons into isolation and being rehabilitated because of it may sound unusual. Since our present rehabilitation methods used in prisons are a failure, the isolation-rehabilitation (Iso-Rehab) program that is proposed should have the full support and endorsement of the government and critics who should want to try a method that would actually work and rehabilitate criminals.

All studies indicate that some form of isolation is beneficial for all criminals, especially for juvenile delinquents. The quicker the juvenile is removed from the family, the neighborhood, the peer pressures, the better the chances that the youth will be reformed and change the behavior patterns. The converse of this premise is also true.

Critics of my plan may feel that isolation is an uncommon form of rehabilitation; however, the present prison rehabilitation programs are failing. Some critics may feel that isolating prisoners is harsh and unusual punishment. Solitary confinement in "the hole" comes to mind when the term isolation is mentioned. It conjures up thoughts of cold, dark, damp dungeons with little or no food and rats gnawing at the prisoners.

In the Iso-Rehab program all of the mean and evil conditions that prisoners are subjected to in our current prisons are removed. There is no punishment in the Iso-Rehab program unless one construes solitude and safety as punishment. It is time for critics to open their minds and give this plan a fair consideration and trial. The results of a fair trial may change their minds to this much needed change.

Consider that it is not punishment:

1. to be safe from sexual assault when showering.

2. to be safe from physical assault and beatings.

3. to be able to eat a meal in peace without having to give some food to some prison ruffian.

4. to be able to sleep without worry of being attacked in bed.

5. to be safe from coercion to join a prison gang.

6. to be provided a secure room in which to rethink and relearn.

7. to be separated from bad, harmful influences.

8. to be given audio instruction and reading material that may actually rehabilitate.

9. to be separated from the criminal training that takes place in the present prisons.

10. to live in a clean room with your own sink, shower, commode, table, and bed.

11. to be able to think and meditate on your life and your future.

12. to learn respect for law and order and moral codes of conduct.

13. to know that once you return to society you will not return to a life of crime.

14. to exercise daily in your own room.

15. to be served three healthy nutritional meals a day.

16. to acquire a better self-image about yourself.

17. to reduce harassment and intimidation.

18. to eliminate the possibility of becoming a drug user.

19. to know upon release you will be safe from any revenge caused by prisoner conflicts.

20. to know you have changed your life and outlook for the better.

Criminologists, sociologists, psychologists, educators, government officials, the general public, and the prisoners themselves must agree that all of the conditions listed would be most beneficial in the prison and the rehabilitation process. Isolation plays a key role here. The reason our current prisons fail is because they have not eliminated the bad factors and have not supplied the good factors.

In a prison setting, the many advantages of isolation can hardly be ignored. Inmates would not have to worry about being attacked, injured, and possibly killed by other inmates. They would be safe from intimidation, badgering, threats, and assault from prison gangs. Segregation and isolation would eliminate sexually-transmitted diseases which seem to be rampant and feared within the prison confines. It would cut prisoners off from the many bad influences that are common to ruffians behind bars. Eliminating these influences would create an atmosphere which would be beneficial to rehabilitation and reeducating criminals which is supposed to be the primary goal of prisons and incarceration.

We know from millions of failed experiments—the ex-convicts who haven't improved their lifestyles once outside and those repeat offenders who end up within the prison system again—that our present form of incarceration and the mixing and mingling of prisoners does not work. Despite the good, humane intentions of our current penal-rehabilitative system: It does not work! We need to try alternative methods if we value the lives and futures of our prisoners and our communities. We need to give isolation-rehabilitation a fair chance.

Goals of Iso-Rehab

1. Do no harm. Do not teach criminals how to be more successful or violent in the world of crime. Do not take a minor, nonviolent offender and return him to society a hardened, violent, and more vicious criminal.

2. Remove the law breakers from society. Provide adequate room to house criminals so that violent convicts are not free to prey upon the community while on probation. Provide adequate room for prisoners so that early parole is not used as simply a way to release one prisoner to make room for another.

3. Insure the safety of prisoners. Protect prisoners from physical and psychological harm from other prisoners as well as over anxious staff and correctional officers.

4. Provide for the health and medical care of prisoners. Prevent physical trauma which is usually caused by the hands of other inmates. Prevent the spread of disease: especially AIDS and other venereal diseases. Prevent the spread of other communicable diseases. Treat and assure treatment is forthcoming for medical problems requiring treatment.

5. Provide for the comfort and feeding of prisoners. A clean room with private toilet facilities and nutritious food must be provided for every prisoner.

6. Provide a safe atmosphere without distractions for purposes of retraining and rehabilitation.

7. Conduct a retraining program that stands a chance of working as compared to our current methods that return dismal results.

8. Provide a cost-effective correctional system.

9. Establish a program that is flexible. A program that can change with the demands of an ever-increasing rate of crime and an increasing rate of violence. A program that can change with the public's demands.

10. To be a state correctional facility free of the problems of county or city/county politics and budgetary restraints at the county level.

The size and scope of the Iso-Rehab program demands that it be controlled and managed by the state. The Iso-Rehab system is dependent upon a stable correctional organization with trained professional correctional workers.

Target Groups of Isolation-Rehabilitation

The Iso-Rehab prison facility can be used for most types of criminals: youths and adults; young and old; male and female; violent and nonviolent. By its mere physical layout, it is a safe place for each and every category of offender. Ideally, it would be considered for offenders that would probably be put at too much risk in the standard prison setting. How often have you heard that violent youth offenders are not placed in the regular prison setting because the authorities fear they can not cope with the violence and the stress of the adult facility? This is an admission that our present prisons are not safe. In Iso-Rehab, each prisoner is physically separated from all other prisoners and is free from any threat of violence or physical harm. In safe surroundings, they are primed and ready for the rehabilitation process.

Let us consider some categories of offenders and how they would benefit from spending their time in an Iso-Rehab prison facility.

Juveniles:

Iso-Rehab segregates the young offenders and keeps them safe from the brutalities and sexual abuse that are common place in standard prisons. This puts them in an ideal, secure environment which allows rehabilitation to take place. They would benefit most from the rehabilitation program because they are young and still impressionable. They can be reprogrammed, through modifications in their behavior, to learn the acceptable rules and regulations of a law-abiding society and its expectations of a young individual. They can be taught that their behavior and attitudes caused their problems, not society or the environment. They can be trained to improve their self-image and thus become a productive member of society.

Other advantages of Iso-Rehab include: training through good examples; not honoring or rewarding misbehavior; teaching accountability, control, and responsibility for one's action; instilling respect for law and order and codes of conduct; and most importantly, respect for oneself. By liking and respecting oneself, one learns to respect others. Today's youngsters harbor too much hate, resentment, and revenge which could be an explanation for the rise in the violent crimes being committed by younger and younger children. Thus, these young offenders are the ideal candidates and would benefit from the Iso-Rehab units and program the most.

Women:

Women inmates need the same security as the youthful offenders. By being in Iso-Rehab, they are free from vicious attacks from other inmates and they are secure in knowing that they will not be sexually violated in the prison setting. First-time female offenders are ideal candidates for the Iso-rehab units and can be reformed through the audio messages that are an integral part of the rehabilitation process and employed in each unit as a method of retraining and reprogramming.

Elderly Inmates:

First-time offenders that are elderly need the same security the Iso-rehab units offer to the female and youthful offenders, and for the same reasons. However, chronic elderly inmates are by their very nature are less able to be rehabilitated and should not take up space that can be used in a more constructive manner. If they were to be in this facility, it would be for safety reasons only.

Policemen:

Often policemen will be convicted of crimes and sentenced to prison. They pose a difficult problem for the correctional facilities. They are at an increased risk of not surviving the violence in our regular prison facilities. They also are a problem for the prison guards who have an alliance with them, but who also have mixed feelings about cops that have gone bad, thus giving law enforcement personnel a bad name.

General Category First-Time Offenders:

Any first-time offender, violent or nonviolent, will be able to benefit from the rehabilitation program inherent in the Iso-Rehab system. The complete program teaches prisoners that they can control their well-being and level of comfort by reforming their present behavior patterns. The Iso-Rehab facility is especially suited, by its rehabilitation program, to accommodate the first-time offenders. They can profit from the safety and the security provided in order to concentrate on the real work of rehabilitation.

The Problem of Overcrowding:

The Iso-Rehab prison facility is the answer to our burgeoning prisoner populations. More often than not, criminals are put back onto the streets, through early release programs, because there is no room in our present prisons. Others are given only probation because of the lack of space. Iso-Rehab allows for the confinement of offenders instead of probation or early release. It also lessens the strain of the parole system. We do not need known offenders out on the streets merely because of overcrowding.

Perhaps the most valuable benefit of the Iso-Rehab facility is its ability to absorb the overflow and overcrowding of our current prison system. With overcrowding there are additional problems which decrease the safety of the staff and prisoners. The tension between guards and prisoners, between prisoners and prisoners, and amongst staff members increases with overcrowding. The awareness of the volatility is felt by the staff and their tension level is increased. To prevent an increase in the number of homicides, assaults, and major disorders, there must be higher and stricter levels of supervision. As with a race car running at full capacity, all systems must be finely tuned and functioning well. The failure of any system will soon be reflected in a breakdown.

Good supervisors that anticipate the problems of over-crowding will have better luck—there is always an element of luck when dealing with criminals—preventing problems than will business-as-usual supervisors. Supervision is the key. A good supervisor will probably have good results and a poor supervisor will probably have poor results. In either case, the prison facility is dependent on, and saddled with, the type of supervisor in charge and the results because of that individual.

The Iso-Rehab units are not affected by the supervisors or the tensions of an overcrowded system to such an extent. First, there is no such thing as overcrowding in an Iso-Rehab facility. The unit is either less than full or it is full. If there is a need for more capacity, then new units are attached to accommodate the increase of prisoners. As long as space is available, units can be added and there will be no problem with overcrowding. Since it is inexpensive to build when compared to standard prison construction, and can be easily expanded, it is ideal to accommodate any overflow of prisoners. It eliminates the need for new, maximum security prisons or facilities of lesser security, which are considered when our current prisons start to overflow. Building the flexible Iso-Rehab models, provides complete prisoner retention plus security for the community, the staff, and the prisoners.

Personnel:

Another prime factor in the correctional equation is the prison staff. The staff of administrators, guards, correctional specialists, and all the ancillary personnel are what make a prison operate. Many of the prison workers are dedicated, hard-working, compassionate employees that are trying to make the system work. There are some business-as-usual, it's-a-job employees that do their job, but could care less. Also there are a few sadistic types that gravitate—or become sadistic after dealing with criminals—to prison work as a release for their inner frustrations.

By and large; however, the staff of our prisons have a tough and thankless job. Prison employees must deal with people most of us would shudder to be near. Murderers, rapists, thugs, sex-offenders, and the very dregs of society must be dealt with on a daily basis. It is no wonder that some correctional people become jaundiced in their outlook.

The beauty of the Iso-Rehab facility is the minimal contact between inmates and the staff. The Iso-Rehab makes the system more foolproof. Any contact is between the staff and a single prisoner, not a yard full of unpredictable miscreants. It eliminates the violence among inmates. It protects the staff and allows them to have more of a one-on-one relationship with each individual prisoner via the continual overhead broadcast programs designed specifically for each prisoner. One-on-one contact between prisoners and staff occurs during the weekly unit inspections. The final results of any program will depend on the prison staff.

Having the prisoners isolated means less personnel which decreases the high costs of staffing. The smaller staff will allow more selectivity when choosing personnel. A smaller staff allows for a close-knit working group that would benefit the overall operation and function of the Iso-Rehab system. Needs of the staff and the prisoners could be more easily met with a smaller, more cohesive correctional force.

Under the Iso-Rehab system, the smaller staff is protected, the prisoners are protected, and the prisoners are controlled—something that few of them have ever experienced and an important step on the road to rehabilitation. Providing this type of protected environment offers the best chance of rehabilitation, which is an added advantage that cannot be overlooked and denied.

Overall, the advantages of the Iso-Rehab system are overwhelming. To consider all aspects of the system: the cost; the ease of building; the flexibility of the system; smaller staff; its safety; and the fact that it has a much better chance of rehabilitating prisoners than our present systems, is to wonder why someone has not proposed this system before now. We need this multi-faceted tool in our correctional arsenal.

Voices from Above

When first entering the Iso-Rehab unit, the prisoner will be handcuffed and blindfolded. The prisoner will then be led to his or her unit. The handcuffs will be removed and the prisoner will be placed inside the unit and the door secured.

One might ask, why do they need handcuffs? The reason is simple. Handcuffs are needed for a psychological factor.

Handcuffing the prisoner before allowing him or her to enter the cell establishes a last minute hands-on control before releasing the prisoner into the cell. The prisoner feels controlled to the very last moment before finding himself completely isolated and under no control, but faced with his own thoughts and self-doubts.

The prisoner will have thoughts about what may happen to him and doubts about his future. Without his peer group to support him the prisoner may doubt the wisdom of his actions that led to crime and eventual incarceration. He will have no one to brag to about his toughness and how mean he is. He will soon realize that his toughness and meanness makes no difference in isolation. He will soon ask himself if it was all worth it.

A person may also question the need for blindfolding or hooding a prisoner. Once again, the answer is to gain a certain psychological advantage. Blindfolding the prisoner prevents him from knowing much about his surroundings. It removes some of the security a prisoner might feel when he knows the layout of the facility. Blindfolding the prisoner will cause the prisoner to worry and have doubts. The prisoner will worry about what his new situation might mean. He will have doubts about what may happen next. At any rate, he will be off balance and receptive to any suggestion that promises stability and security. The simple act of blindfolding will get the prisoners' attention. Once you have the attention of the prisoner, the rehabilitation process can begin.

It is essential to make the prisoner feel alone, apprehensive, and expectant. When the prisoner feels this way, he will grasp at messages that add form and structure to his thoughts. He will listen to and follow directions if by so doing he adds to his own well-being. Blindfolding a prisoner for the few minutes it takes to transfer him into his cell will make him attentive to the first messages. The prisoner in total isolation and without any outside stimuli or distractions for the first few hours will be primed and ready for the sound of a human voice.

The first few hours in isolation will be a shock to the gangsters and criminals who have thrived on the support of their peers. Most gang members feel lost and inadequate without the gang support. Gangsters are not very impressive when they lose the comfort and assurance of their fellow mobsters. Yes, the first few hours in total isolation will be a shock to their systems—a shock similar to that of a dope addict cut off from his drug source.

It does not take long for the tough guy syndrome to leave when there is nobody around to bully and to impress with toughness. Total isolation can change a persons' outlook rapidly. It is with the initial change in a prisoners' outlook that *voices from above*—the audio messages piped into the cell through a ceiling speaker—can affect a change in a prisoners' thinking. First impressions are generally very important and long lasting. It is important that the first messages the prisoner receives are strongly stated and make a lasting impression.

The first message will welcome the prisoner to his cell unit. This message will establish the ground rules and the expected behavior. It will also mention what penalties they might expect when the rules are broken. It will explain the proper use of the wash basin, the commode, and the shower. It will also tell the prisoner that he will get his first meal when he places his blindfold or hood—whichever was used—into the food tray slot. The first message will emphasize that if the blindfold or hood is not put in the food tray slot then the prisoner will receive no meal.

Overhead Message Example 1:

A sample introductory message that would be aired to the prisoner:

Welcome (John Didwrong) to your unit in the Iso-Rehab facility. You will be safe here during your stay. Relax. Set aside your worries and listen to what I'm going to tell you. It'll make your stay here easier. You have probably asked yourself many times; Why am I here? What did I do that caused me to be in this place? You will have plenty of time to ask yourself that and other questions later. Right now, let me explain your present situation and the rules you must follow while you are in your Iso-Rehab unit.

First of all, you are safe here in your unit. No one will hurt you. This is your room where you will stay. Notice how nice and clean your room is. You will want to keep your room clean. It is nicer to live in a clean, dry room than a dirty, wet room.

You can see that your room has a sink and a toilet. These are operated by the push buttons near them. The shower has no such button because we will tell you when to take a shower. We will turn the water on and off for you. We'll explain this later. All these facilities are clean and in good working order. Keep them that way. We know that you could clog the toilet.

If you do clog the toilet, you will have to live in a wet, smelly room from the water and sewage on the floor. That would not be comfortable for you. It is best to keep your room clean and comfortable. By the way (John Didwrong), if you are thirsty you can use the plastic cup that is next to the wash basin for a drink of water.

You can see that you have a towel and wash cloth. You can exchange the towel, the wash cloth, and your clothes for clean items on the laundry exchange day. You will be reminded before the exchange takes place. Remember, in order to receive clean items you must return the dirty ones through the slot when instructed. This policy of exchange will hold true for all items that you use.

You were blindfolded when you entered your room. Put the blindfold in the slot near the door. That slot is the food tray slot. You will get your meals through that slot three times a day. You will exchange all items through that slot. To get your first meal you must place your blindfold in that slot.

Your meal tray will contain your food along with a plastic spoon. The first meal tray will contain other items also: A toothbrush and toothpaste for you to use and keep in your room. Each morning you will receive a packet of toilet paper. After you eat, you must return the tray, the spoon, and the empty plastic items in the food tray slot to receive your next meal. If you do not return your tray, spoon, and dishes you will not get your next meal. This is important to understand and remember.

At certain times your meal tray will contain other items. As an example, on shower days, every two days, you will receive a small bottle or packet of soap and a disposable razor, both of which you must return on the next tray after use. Remember, in order to get things, you must return things. Otherwise, you will deprive yourself of these things. It's a very simple rule to understand and follow. Periodically, we will remind you. We are here to help and protect you.

Have you thought of why you were sentenced to spend time here in the Iso-Rehab? You know why. Think about it. You did something that was wrong. That is why you are here. Think what you did. You will have plenty of time to think about it.

By the way, your mattress pad and fold-over blanket should be warm enough for you. There is a seat at the end of the bed and a table so you can eat your meal. I hope you are comfortable. I will leave you now. In the meantime, think back over what you did and why you are here. Remember to pay close attention and follow all the instructions that you will be hearing. Remember, your own character makes or breaks you. I'll talk to you later. Put your blindfold in the slot so you can get your meal. Bye for now.

Overhead Message Example 2:

Sample instructional message aired throughout the day:

Attention Inmates. In fifteen minutes there will be an exercise program. I'll announce the exercises and count the number of times you should be able to perform each exercise. The exercises will include sit-ups, push-ups, squats, and jumping jacks. Painted and imprinted on the wall opposite your bed are pictured the exercises and how to properly perform them.

I'll vary the exercise sequence, the number of repetitions, and the speed of the exercises. There will be three exercise periods a day for fifteen minutes each time. Hope you are able to join in, follow along, and keep up with the exercises. Talk to you soon.

Overhead Message Example 3

Example of an individualized message for inmate "John Didwrong":

Hi John, hope you are doing okay. What are you thinking about? I bet you are wondering what we are going to do to you here. Do not worry because we are not going to harm you in any way. The only one that can make your life more difficult is you, yourself. Think about it. We are going to help you improve your life. Listen to what we will tell you and you will not make the same mistakes again. Don't give up hope.

First, you must realize that your behavior and what you did is bad. Really bad. John, did anyone ever tell you about the Ten Commandments? They are rules to live by. They are laws of conduct. Most major religions have rules and laws that people should live by if they are going to be safe and happy. The laws can be explained by what some people have called the "Golden Rule"—*Do unto others as you would have them do unto you.* In other words John, treat other people like you would want them to treat you. Easy isn't it? If you want a friend then you should treat that person friendly and be nice to them. They will respond by treating you nicely. You will have a friend.

Some of the commandments and laws of religion have become our laws; such as, Thou shall not kill. John, you broke that law—that is the reason you are here. Another commandment says; Thou shall not steal. You know what that means. If something is not yours, leave it alone, do not take it. Thou shall not lie is another law. It is always best to tell the truth. If you lie to someone they probably know you are lying. Then one lie leads to another, and so on; sooner or later, after many lies, the truth will come out. So, John, make sure you tell the truth the first chance you get or you will be caught up in a pack of lies. And John, you know how bad you feel when someone catches you lying. John, always tell the truth.

John, do you feel sorry for what you did to Mary? Do you feel sad that her mother and father cry because she is no longer with them? It's okay to feel sad about something wrong that you have done. You should promise that you will never do anything bad again.

John, how would you feel if someone killed your mother? How would you want to treat them? How do you think you should be treated?

Later this afternoon, you will be told when the shower will be turned on. It will only be on for about seven minutes. Be ready to step into the shower as soon as it starts. That way, you will not miss or lose any of your shower time. Bye for now, John. By the way, were you able to follow and keep up with the exercises earlier? Talk to you later. Bye for now John.

The foregoing three messages are examples of the audio program that will be aired through the units' ceiling speakers many times a day. Each prisoner will have messages tailored specifically for his or her particular situation. The messages will be as varied and as different as the prison population demands. The use of female voices will be used for certain messages to portray a mother image for an inmate. Where applicable, ethnic voices and idiom can be used to enforce or clarify a message. As one can see, the variations and messages are endless.

There will be messages telling of food, shower time, and instructions concerning clean clothes and linen exchanges. Messages will announce the exercise times and the exercises to be performed. The exercises will be described in detail and cadence will be counted during the exercise.

Initially, there will be at least three messages each hour between 6AM and 6PM specifically aimed at each inmates' crime and the steps to take to correct the criminal behavior. These specific messages will be reduced over time to one message, concerning the specific inmates' crime, every hour.

Education messages will be presented at a future date to teach a variety of subjects. Soft, background music will be played over the unit speaker in between the specific criminal messages and the educational programs.

The messages will be developed by the Iso-Rehab psychologist and the message team. The size of the team is dictated by the workload and the number of prisoners. The message team would function similarly to a disc jockey. Each member of the message team would announce specific messages prescribed by the team leader—the Iso-Rehab psychologist.

Dealing with Problems

One can foresee certain problems with any system. The possible problems anticipated with the Iso-Rehab system are all inmate-generated. Prisoners are not nice people or they wouldn't be in the program in the first place. They will try to beat-the-system and gain advantages whenever and wherever they can. The below mentioned scenarios are by no means the complete list of possible problems—they are merely examples of what might happen. The inmates will be made aware of these consequences upon their arrival and throughout their stay.

The solution proposed for each of the listed problem scenes is consistent with the overall plan and approach of the Iso-Rehab system; that is, never give in to misconduct. Ceding to a prisoners' bad behavior only reinforces the bad behavior. Furthermore, worsening of the prisoners' condition is caused by the prisoner and not the system. Therefore, any problems that result because of the inmates' disobedience or misconduct are self-inflicted.

The prisoners soon learn—if we do not give in—that they are responsible for their own well-being during their tour in the Iso-Rehab units. They can make themselves miserable by misconduct or improve their conditions by behaving and fol-lowing the rules. In either case, they are learning that they are responsible for their own fate. This learning is inner-directed and helps the inmate to become a more responsible, account-able individual.

Clogging the Toilet:

A prisoner might clog the commode with a towel or clothing. The resulting overflow of sewage would make life more difficult for the prisoner; however, no immediate action would be taken. The prisoner would not receive his next meal, and the prisoner would have to live in the self-made mess for at least two days after which the problem would be solved and the unit sterilized. The prisoner could be moved to another unit during the clean-up process. No advantage or disadvantage would be gained since all the units are identical. If the prisoner continued to clog the commode, then each offense would earn an additional day in the mess before clean-up.

Not Returning Food Trays:

Food trays are brought to the prisoners' unit three times a day. The instructions given upon admission to the system and reiterated through the overhead broadcasts each day, state that empty food trays, plus the plastic spoon they got with the last meal, must be in the tray slot in order to receive the subsequent meal and before the next meal tray is delivered. A simple, understandable, regulation: In order to get a meal, return the tray in the prescribed time. The breakfast tray in the slot by the time the lunch tray is delivered and so on. If the breakfast tray is not presented in the units' tray slot when the lunch tray arrives—the prisoner will simply miss that meal. This principle will follow with each meal.

The scenario of missing meals could go on indefinitely or until the prisoner either died of starvation or started to accept the responsibility of feeding himself and exchanging a tray for another meal. In any event, the inmate is responsible for the outcome. He is accountable for his own action. The opportunity is there to eat and feed himself, he can blame no one except himself for not receiving food.

Screaming and Hollering:

Each unit, though not soundproof, is resistant to sound transmission. Any inmate who screams and hollers is making his unit more unpleasant for himself. Prisoners have been instructed that no one will respond to the screams and noise that the prisoners may make. He is there to think and ponder. Perhaps after carrying on in such a manner he will feel rather foolish. The prisoners' voice and vocal cords will play out in a short period of time. He soon learns that there is no form of misconduct that will be rewarded. Here again, the prisoner experiences learning from within himself. No one has to teach the inmate that screaming and hollering will make him hoarse or that by stopping the noise his situation will improve. It is the old touch-the-hot-stove-once lesson.

Any number of problem scenarios could be developed herein to cover a myriad of incidents. The result will always be the same. Misbehavior will get no immediate attention or recognition. Any problem behavior goes without reward. If the prisoner chooses to act in an unacceptable manner, he will only hurt himself because he has to deal with the problem he himself created. Soon he will learn to behave because he is responsible for the outcome of his actions. He learns to be accountable for whatever he chooses to do. Most importantly, he learns that there is no one to blame but himself. Thus, over time, the prisoner rewards himself with good behavior.

Chapter Eight

Structure and Design Plans

Prison Structure and Design

Today, the United States has enormous prisons that are very costly to build, costly to maintain, and costly to supervise and guard. Traditional prisons are built much the same as they were over a hundred years ago. The traditional prison is a monstrosity and requires huge plots of land and is time-consuming to build. The very nature of the traditional prison requires a large administrative staff, numerous security personnel, and correctional officers. A prison building is either part of the solution or part of the problem. Our present prison buildings are part of the problem.

The layout of the traditional prison is cumbersome and does not lend itself to easy prisoner movement and prisoner control. Huge exercise yards, large dining halls, and large bathing areas are almost impossible to control. These areas are breeding grounds for violence and the breakdown of security. Large dining halls require extensive areas devoted to food handling, food storage, and food preparation. There is almost no security in any of these areas. The shower facilities are poorly secured and present opportunities for violence and sexual assault. The yard is the enclosure that allows prisoners to mill around and form cliques and gangs. This is where convicts can plan strikes, breakouts, escapes, and run the prison hustle. The Iso-Rehab design uses the structure of the prison as an integral part of the control and management of the prisoners. By the very layout of the prison building, prisoner movement and control is simplified. The building lends itself to the control of the prisoners and requires a very small staff to operate when compared with the traditional prison.

The nation is full of enormous prison facilities that are inefficient, poorly designed, and ill-suited for the safety and rehabilitation of prisoners. This chapter explores a different type of prison construction. The design is a modular type prison structure. It creates a prison that is easy to maintain, to secure, and requires minimal personnel to operate. It can be easily expanded to accommodate more inmates. It includes a prison program that fits in well with the reeducation and possible rehabilitation of the convicts. The structure and design is an essential part of the rehabilitation program used to teach or rehabilitate the prisoners. This prison is inexpensive by todays' standards and is suited to the philosophy and the goals of correction.

This new concept creates a prison that can accept all types of prisoners. Youthful offenders, female inmates, adult male prisoners, and various other types of convicts can be housed in the same facility. No special accommodations need be made for the various categories of prisoners.

The prison described herein provides all the necessary comforts with one big advantage: It provides a level of safety here-to-fore unknown in our prisons. The Iso-Rehab construction provides solitary comfort and security. The peace and quiet will augment the retraining program. The psychological training techniques will help the prisoners modify their behavior to their own benefit. This prison provides a safe atmosphere in which to live and in which to accept training that leads to true rehabilitation. All in all, this new prison protects the prisoners, it protects the guards, and it actually provides the necessary conditions for the retraining, and perhaps the rehabilitation of prisoners.

Site Location

A vacant or open area in an existing prison facility is a possible location for an Iso-Rehab facility. It could function to alleviate many of the problems plaguing the current prisons. Staff and other ancillary services could be shared between the prison and the Iso-Rehab facility. Land acquisition, and the many obstacles of trying to create a free-standing correctional facility would be solved by placing the Iso-Rehab on existing prison grounds. The two systems could develop a symbiotic relationship and save millions of dollars.

If the Iso-Rehab facility is placed in an existing prison complex it is imperative that it be autonomous. Without autonomy, the Iso-Rehab would be usurped by the prison and become another isolation cell in the prison complex. It is also important that the facility functions independently, and is self-governing.

As a free-standing facility, the Iso-Rehab facility can accommodate 520 prisoners on a five-acre plot. The usual problems of land acquisition, citizen approval, transportation, and utilities would need to be addressed.

Plot and Placement Considerations

The prime requirement for a construction site is a level area, not in a flood plain or subject to flooding or swamping during heavy rains and snows. The area needed for the construction site depends on two things:

1. the size of the facility being built initially;and

2. future anticipated needs for possible expansion.

Proposed layouts and plans for the Iso-Rehab facility (refer to Diagrams C and D), can house 160 inmates on a one-acre plot of ground. Given these proposals, a five-acre plot of ground could accommodate 520 inmates with enough room for support facilities.

Ideally, the Iso-Rehab facility would be built away from any city or residential area. An acceptable location would be a remote country area at least five miles distance from a small farming town. Leasing a five-acre plot in the middle of a dry land wheat section would be ideal for those of us who live in the plains states. Other, equally satisfactory, sites can be developed in every state in the union.

Requirements for whatever site is chosen are:

1. access by a hard-surfaced road;

2. helicopter access;

3. availability of electric power;

4. telephone transmission;

5. an adequate supply of potable water; and

6. adequate drainage of the site.

Sewage and biodegradable waste can be handled in a number of ways. Leaching fields, composting pits and fields, and bacteria consumption pits are all viable options for dealing with the generated wastes. These waste options have been used successfully for progressive small cities and towns in America. They are environmentally friendly.

Pod Foundation Preparation

The basic unit of the Iso-Rehab facility is the Pod (refer to Diagram B for Single Pod). The Pod has two, twenty-unit rows serviced by a maintenance alley. The maintenance alley is the area that requires excavation prior to the actual pouring of the concrete pad upon which the units will be attached. *Figure A-1* depicts a cross section of the maintenance alley excavation.

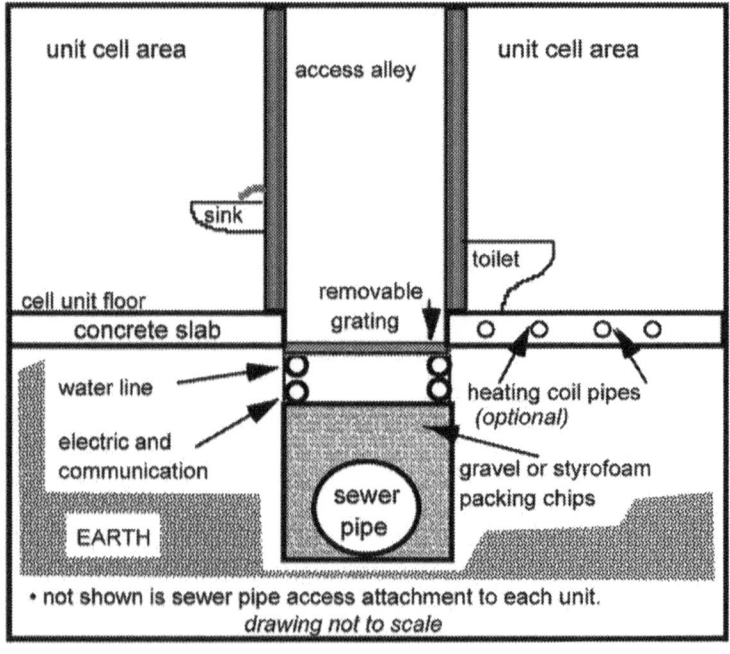

Figure A-1: Cross section of maintenance alley

Foundation

The foundation is a six-inch concrete slab with optional heating coils imbedded. This type of slab has been used for years and has proven successful for driveways and various warehouse applications. This substructure can be poured in place or purchased as a prestressed concrete slab. Each section of foundation slab will have preset bolts imbedded to secure the separate units in place. There will also be large bolts imbedded around the perimeter to secure the peripheral walls. An added bonus of the bolt-down and screw-together construction is that it can be easily unbolted, unscrewed, and taken apart. It can be expanded and contracted.

Peripheral Walls:

Constructed of prestressed concrete, in twenty-foot sections, able to be bolted to the foundation and moved for expansion purposes in the future if necessary. Each twenty-foot wall section will be fourteen-feet high and will be able to support an all-weather roof. Additionally, there will be halogen floodlights on the interior and exterior perimeters positioned to brightly illuminate both sides of the peripheral walls. Video cameras will be positioned both inside and outside the peripheral walls as well as along the various service rows.

Roof:

An all-weather insulated roof can be erected that can be incorporated with the peripheral walls. The roof can be supported by steel posts similar to many warehouse roofs. Air vents and skylights can be part of the roof. Ceiling lights and heating devices can be hung from the roof superstructure as well as fans for cooling.

Plumbing:

Plumbing for water service and sewage disposal will access each unit via the four-foot maintenance alleys that extend the length of the Pod. The sewer lines are the only utility requiring presetting or excavation prior to pouring the concrete slab or setting the slab in place. See *Figure A-1* for water and sewer access.

Electricity:

Each unit will receive electricity via the maintenance alley. Electricity will power the lights, sound system, and back-up heating supply. The lighting for each unit will be supplied by two, four-foot fluorescent tubes recessed in the ceiling and protected by high-strength transparent Plexiglas. Lighting will be controlled from the guard station, not by the inmate from within the unit. An auxiliary electric power generating system will be available in case of an electric power failure.

The sound system will be "piped-in" from the recessed ceiling speaker with appropriate protective covering. All sound will be controlled from the educational-rehabilitation office, and the guard office.

Toilet Facilities:

The back wall of each unit will have a built-in stainless steel sink-commode combination. This combined unit will have controlled flusher and faucet push buttons. A built-in shower stall with no controls will also be on the back wall. The shower's flow and water temperature will be centrally controlled from the rehabilitation office which will advise the prisoner of the shower time and duration prior to the water flowing. On shower days, three-times-a-week, a small plastic packet of liquid soap and razor will be included on the food tray along with a wash cloth, towel, and change of clothes. All shower

Alone To Think

items will be returned when the next meal tray is distributed or the prisoner will receive no meal.

Exercise Area:

Each unit is designed with an open floor space of approximately seven-feet by five-and-a-half-feet to allow for exercise. Calisthenics, including jumping jacks, push-ups, alternate lunges, squats, and sit-ups could be performed very easily in this area.

Bed-Seat-Table:

Built into one side wall will be a bed platform thirty-inches wide by seven-feet long which will stand fifteen inches above the concrete floor. At one end of the bed platform, and built into the bed structure itself, will be a reinforced area of approximately eighteen-inches by thirty-inches, the same width of the bed platform, that will serve as a seat and also can double as a head rest for sleep. The seat portion of the bed structure will fit comfortably under the built-in table platform, one-foot wide by thirty-inches long, which extends from the adjacent shower stall. The mattress will be a preformed foam cushion with an elevated area to serve as a pillow and seat.

Access Door:

The wall opposite the wall that contains the sink-commode combination and shower stall will house the unit access door. The door will open outwards and will be smooth on the inside. It will be of heavy-duty steel with hinges on the outside. An one-foot square, one-way mirror will be in the center of the door, five-feet above floor level. This one-way mirror will allow staff to look into the cell from the outside, but the prisoner will only see his reflection in the mirror. An electronic latch will be used with each door-locking mechanism and be relayed to a display panel in the guard station.

Food Tray Slot:

On the same wall as the door, there will be a food tray slot measuring fifteen inches by four inches which would be at floor level. Three-times-a-day; breakfast, lunch, and dinner trays are passed through the slot in exchange for the tray from the previous meal. A plastic spoon will be included with each meal tray, but must be accounted for in the tray exchange. Clothing and linen will also be exchanged through this slot.

The food distribution will be under the control of the prison staff. All meals will be scientifically prepared to insure every prisoner the proper amount of essential vitamins, minerals, and nutrients. Emphasis will be placed on low-fat, high-bulk meals to provide excellent nutrition. It will be provided by civilian contract kitchens, similar to airline meal caterers, through competitive contract bids. The food will be inspected daily by an on-premise dietitian who will help conduct the food distribution. Food trays will be stored in mobile, self-contained service carts similar to the type used on airlines for food and beverage service. Each cart can easily carry enough meals for a Pod of 40 units.

In the event that the Iso-Rehab facility is placed within an existing prison complex, then food trays will be prepared by the prison staff. The meals will then be transported to the Iso-Rehab guard office for meal distribution.

Unit Wall Construction

There are many options for constructing the walls of each unit. Traditional construction has been brick, concrete, cinder block, and some form of metal. The cost of these materials is high and they do not lend themselves to modular flexibility and ease of erection. For this reason, the Iso-Rehab will use two-inch by six-inch construction lumber on twelve-inch centers with three-quarter-inch plywood surfacing. The plywood will be attached with countersunk two-inch self-tapping screws.

The walls will be insulated. They can be easily fabricated in a shop and transported to the construction site and bolted into position. The walls will be oil-treated, painted, plain, or covered with an epoxy coating. The walls will be fireproofed with one of the available products.

The back wall, which accommodates the sink-commode unit and the shower stall, will be built with the proper access ports for water and sewer. The shower stall will have a fiberglass-epoxy lining.

The unit door is in the front wall which will be constructed of two-inch by six-inch lumber with a steel casement incorporated and bolted to the two-inch by six-inch studs. The door itself will be of steel and fitted with a standard electronic prison door lock with a bolt closure. A square-foot, reinforced, one-way mirror will be at eye level. Each door will be controlled from the guard station and also by a special pass key.

Unit Ceiling Construction

The ceiling of a unit will be bolted into place atop the walls. The ceiling contains several important features. An overhead radiant electric heater will be used to supplement the heat from the concrete floor slab. The lighting for the unit will be supplied by two florescent bulbs that will be imbedded in the ceiling and protected by a translucent lamp guard. The overhead speakers will also be imbedded in the ceiling and protected by tamperproof guards. A fresh air vent with guard screen will be built into the ceiling. It is easily connected to an overhead fresh air source. All of these appliances will have dedicated electrical wiring in place with electric plugs for easy connection to the system. A fire-sprinkler system, and a smoke detector will be installed in the ceiling of each unit. A fan will be placed in a central position to be used for cooling as needed.

Each unit ceiling will be compatible with, and easily interchanged with any other unit. The top of the walls will be covered with an half-inch rubberoid cushion that makes a seal when the ceiling is attached and bolted in place. The ceiling unit will be covered with an acoustic covering. Each wall has two built-in bolts that mesh with the bolt holes in the ceiling. The holes are slightly over size to facilitate alignment and placement during the attachment.

Following are diagrams of the proposed designs used in construction of the Iso-Rehab facility.

•*DIAGRAM A*

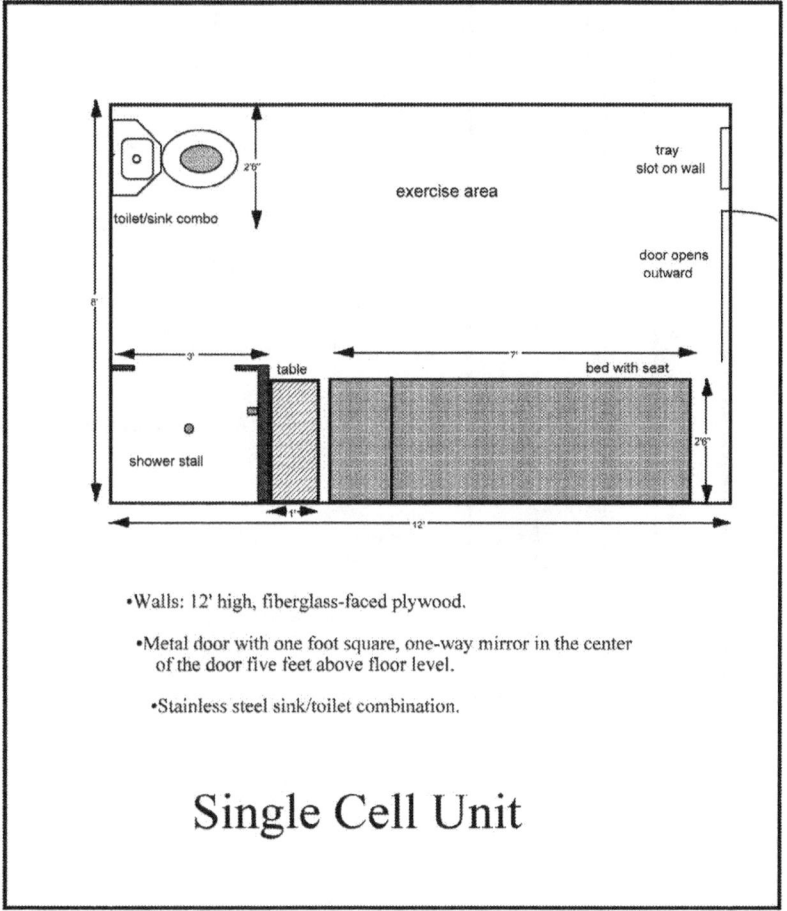

- •Walls: 12' high, fiberglass-faced plywood.

  - •Metal door with one foot square, one-way mirror in the center of the door five feet above floor level.

  - •Stainless steel sink/toilet combination.

Single Cell Unit

Diagram A: Single Cell Unit

•DIAGRAM B

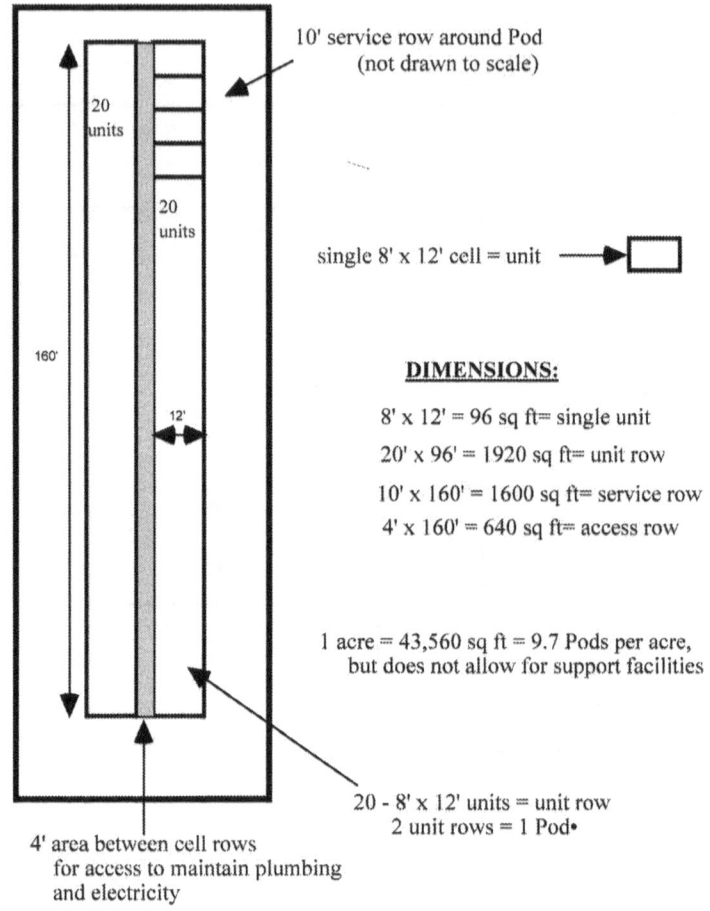

10' service row around Pod
(not drawn to scale)

single 8' x 12' cell = unit

DIMENSIONS:

8' x 12' = 96 sq ft= single unit

20' x 96' = 1920 sq ft= unit row

10' x 160' = 1600 sq ft= service row

4' x 160' = 640 sq ft= access row

1 acre = 43,560 sq ft = 9.7 Pods per acre,
but does not allow for support facilities

20 - 8' x 12' units = unit row
2 unit rows = 1 Pod•

4' area between cell rows
for access to maintain plumbing
and electricity

Single Pod

•40 - 8' x 12' units = 1 Pod = 4480 sq ft•

Diagram B: Single Pod

•DIAGRAM C

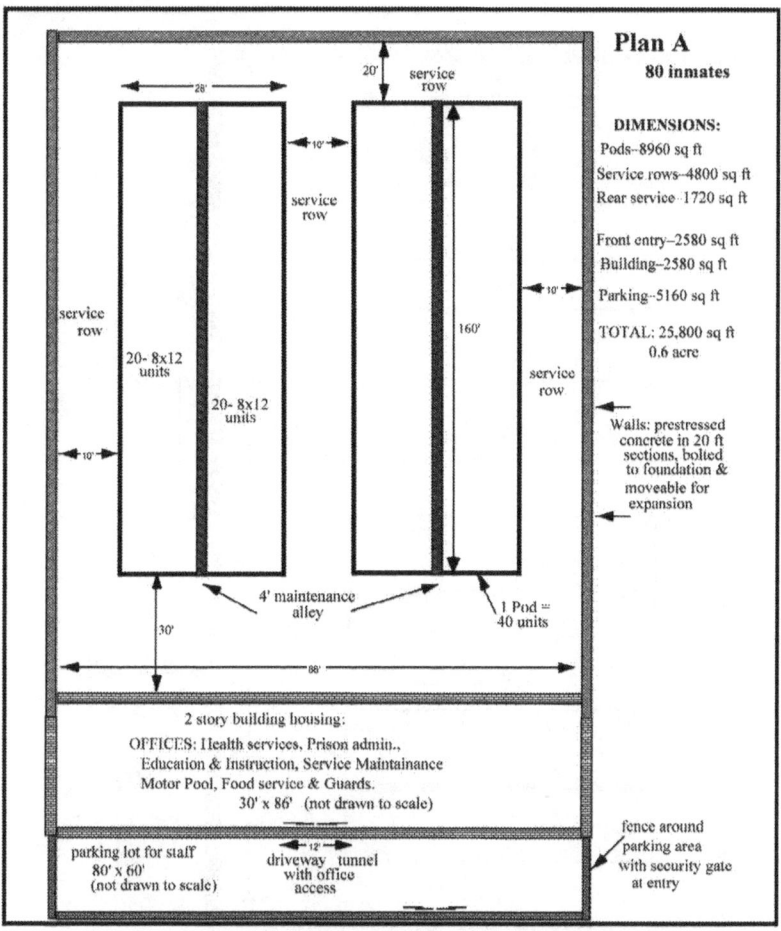

Diagram C: Plan A - 80 inmates

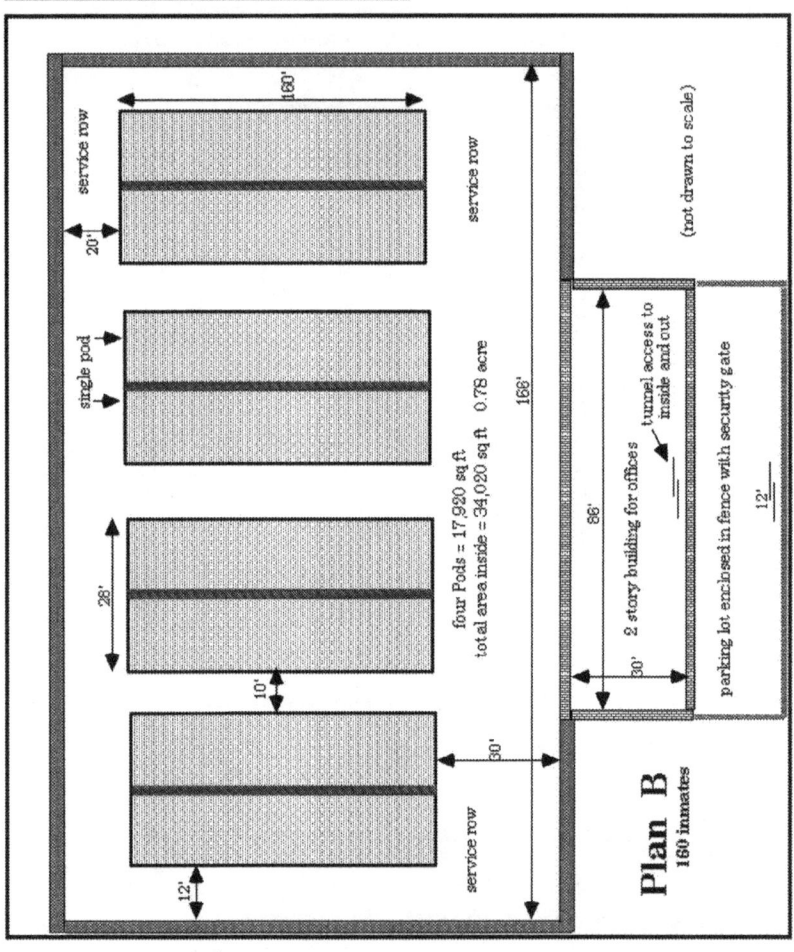

• *DIAGRAM D*

Diagram D: Plan B - 160 inmates

• DIAGRAM E

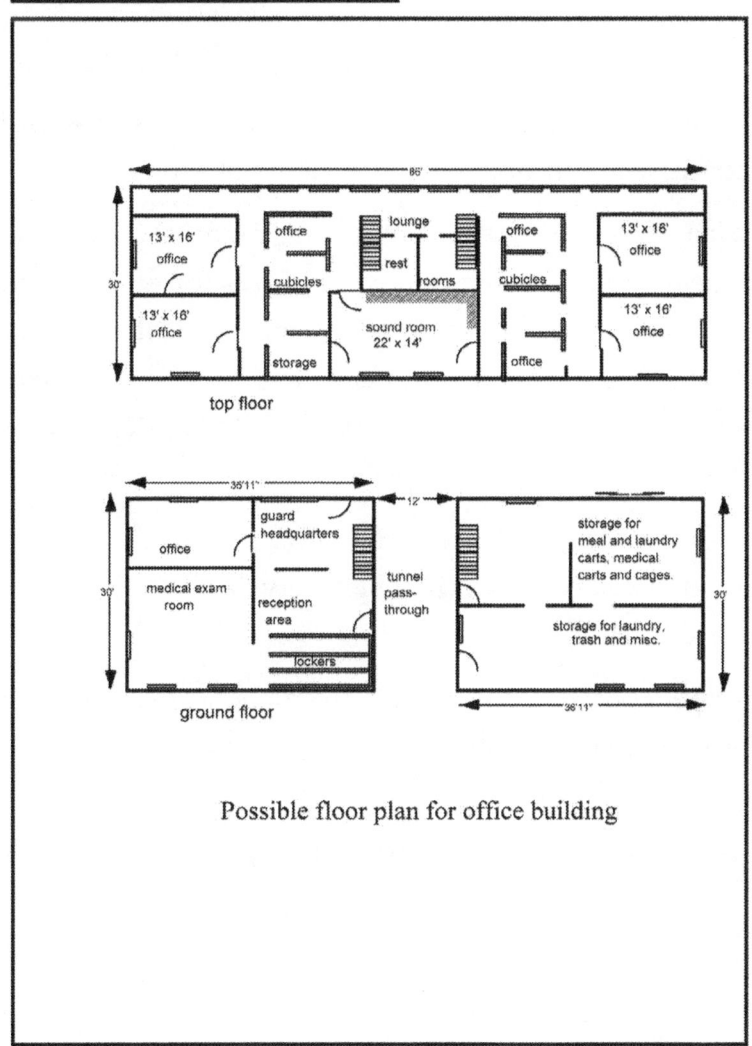

Possible floor plan for office building

Diagram E: Office Building Plan

Terminology for Iso-Rehab Diagrams

unit- single eight-foot by twelve-foot room; 96 sq. ft.

unit row- twenty units all facing a service aisle; 1920 sq. ft.

maintenance alley- four-foot row behind and between two unit rows; 640 sq. ft. This access aisle provides space for the electrical and plumbing requirements of each cell.

service row- ten-foot aisle running along the front side of two unit rows. The service row allows for entrance to the units, food distribution, inspection, medical exam space, and cleaning access to the cells. The service rows expand to twenty-feet on the ends of the Pods to facilitate turning a vehicle.

Pod- two unit rows placed back to back with their maintenance access sandwiched between them; 4,480 sq. ft.; Total 40 units.

Pod square- two Pods, across from each other, sharing the same center service row.

Pod row- Pod units aligned in a row. A two-Pod row contain 80 units; a three-Pod row 120 units, etc....

Estimated Construction Costs

Plan B—160 Inmates

- **Super structure: Pad with roof: 166 ft. wide by 210 ft. long @ $25/sq. ft.:** $871,500.00
- **Lumber for unit cells:** $162,926.00
- **Sink, commode, shower@ $1200/cell unit:**   <u>$192,000.00</u>

	Total:	$1,226,426.00

•Fixtures for ceiling:

Lights—40 watt fluorescent: $53@	$8,480.00
Intercom speaker: $60@	$9,600.00
Sound system console and amplifiers:	$4,000.00
Electric heater: $68@	$10,880.00
Sprinkler: $49@	$7,840.00
Fan—9": $30@	$4,800.00
Electric wiring:	<u>$5,000.00</u>
Total:	$50,600.00

•Plumbing and Sewer:

Sewer line—4" PCP, 20 ft. $12@	$500.00
Drain connectors PCP $30/cell unit	$4800.00
Plumbing:	<u>$24,000.00</u>
Total:	$29,300.00

Estimated Total of Items: *$1,306,326.00*

The cost of an Administration building plus facilities and incidental cost overruns $2,217,663.00, which brings the total cost to $3.5 million. With the construction philosophy of Iso-Rehab, a 160-bed prison facility can be built for $3.5 million. This can keep 160 prisoners for under $1 million a year.

•A 320-bed prison facility can be built for $6 million, which would house 320 prisoners for under $2 million a year.

•Estimated cost to build 2500-bed Iso-Rehab facility would be $46.8 million. Estimated yearly cost to maintain these 2500 prisoners would be $20 million.

Chapter Nine

Staffing

Necessary Personnel

By the very nature of the Iso-Rehab facility, the staffing is reduced. There are no tower guards. Gone are the guards that patrol the yard, the food service area, and the prison industry complex. Removing the prisoners from the danger of the prison industry, the yard, the shower point, and the dining room will reduce emergency medical needs. There is no need to move prisoners from their cells to the dining hall or to the shower area. The prisoners shower, eat, and exercise in the privacy of their cell units. All the inmates are tucked safely away in their private cells. They are safe from harm. Telephone and television repair will be zero since these items are not allowed in the prisoner enclosures.

Specific staff requirements are as follows:

Administration:

The chief administrator must be a person with prison experience. A person who is open-minded and knowledgeable about the prison programs that work and the programs that have failed. Since most programs have failed, the chief administrator must have a let's-try-something-different attitude. Above all, the chief administrator must be devoted to the philosophy of the Iso-Rehab program. He must be able to sell the Iso-Rehab philosophy to his staff and secure the loyalty of every staff member.

The chief administrator must have the tact and the ability to deal with politicians and the local community. A chief must coordinate the staff and control the day-to-day functions of the facility. The chief will oversee the arrival and release of all prisoners and set policy for prisoner visits and prisoner evaluation.

Business Office Staff:

All businesses and organizations need an office staff to manage payroll, employee records, health and insurance, and correspondence. The Iso-Rehab office will manage all employee-related affairs as well as the operating expenses of the facility.

Security Guards:

The guard personnel will be responsible for the security of the Iso-Rehab facility. They will secure the parking lot, the employee work stations, the inmate enclosure areas, and the entire physical structure of the facility.

There will be a chief or head guard who will formulate and enforce the standard guard policy of the facility. The chief will manage the guard schedule and ensure adequate security coverage. Since the Iso-Rehab facility is in operation twenty-four-hours-a-day and every day of the year, there will be three, eight-hour shifts each day. Each shift will have a guard in charge and an adequate number of security officers to handle the workload. There will have to be sufficient personnel to manage three-shifts-a-day, seven-days-a-week, and provide for weekend and vacation coverage.

Guards will accompany and oversee meal distribution and pick up. They will oversee trash and laundry transport to-and-from the facility. The guards will accompany the cell-cleaning detail to control the prisoner while the room is being cleaned. Guards will also make periodic visual inspections of each inmate unit.

Food Service:

Since food is not prepared in the Iso-Rehab facility, the only food personnel support would be administrative. The food manager should be a registered dietitian who will be responsible for the daily and weekly menu plan. The food manager would be responsible for ordering meals, storing meals, and controlling the distribution of meals to the inmates. The food manager will contract with the local food supplier.

In the event that a meal preparation service is added to the Iso-Rehab facility, then the food manager will act as the overseer of this service. A three-day emergency supply of MREs—Meals Ready to Eat—will be kept in locked storage. These meals are standard field rations as well as an emergency food source for the American Armed Forces.

Clothing and Laundry:

Private, off-site, laundry services will be used for all laundry requirements. A clothing manager will be in charge of ordering wash cloths, towels, bed clothes, and clothing for the inmates. The manager will control clothing and laundry distribution and exchange, as well as monitor the condition of the clothing and the bath ensembles. The clothing manager will also be in charge of the storage of all laundry items, along with the laundry reception and removal from the facility. This person will also be part of the meal tray distribution and exchange team.

Staff Psychologist:

There will be a staff psychologist present and on duty daily. The staff psychologist will have a team of workers that will evaluate crime histories and determine the message program to be used for each inmate. The psychology team will be responsible for developing taped messages and broadcast times. They will also develop and air educational programs. The psychology team, in coordination with the chief administrator, will be responsible for evaluating the Iso-Rehab program.

Medical Support:

Assaults, bodily injury, and accidental trauma will be almost nonexistent in the Iso-Rehab facility. There will be no industrial injuries or sexual assault injuries. There will be sickness and nontraumatic medical emergencies such as acute appendicitis, infections, and heart problems. Inmates will be treated similarly to the general public with regards to these illnesses. The inmate will either have to be transported to an emergency department or be seen in the facility by a private "on call" physician.

Upon admission and every three months, each inmate will have a medical exam. Inmates will be evaluated for medical problems. A medical support treatment room, equipped with standard physical exam equipment, including a twelve-lead EKG, emergency intravenous solutions, and oxygen will be maintained. The medical treatment room will contain no narcotics. Simple, over-the-counter medications for headaches, upset stomachs, constipation, and minor skin problems will be available. The medical treatment room will be controlled by the facility doctor-in-charge or the physician assistant-in-charge. A female nurse will be in attendance during any examination or treatment of a female inmate.

Maintenance and Cleaning:

A maintenance man, trained in plumbing and electrical troubleshooting will be in attendance. The maintenance man will be a member of the feeding, laundry, and cleaning team. There will be cleaning employees who will be responsible for the cleaning of the offices, the storage rooms, the parking areas, and the main facility itself.

This team will schedule a weekly cleaning visit to each inmates' room. Cleaning of the inmates' quarters will consist of scouring and disinfecting the basin, the commode, and the shower stall. A portable wet-dry vacuum will be used to clean the floor of the inmates' quarters. During the cleaning operation, the prisoner will be removed from his room and controlled by the guards that accompany the cleaning detail. No more than ten minutes should be required to clean each room, control and secure the inmate, and move to the next cell. Every two weeks, during this procedure, the bed clothes will be changed.

Fire Control:

Fire extinguishers and fire hoses are located at the end of each Pod. Fire extinguishers are also located at strategic points throughout the administration building. The security forces will act as firemen in the event of a fire.

Transportation:

A vehicle operator, capable of driving a truck or a bus will be on duty daily. This person will double as part of the maintenance, food delivery, laundry, and clean-up teams when not driving or servicing a vehicle.

Conclusion

The proper role of government in civilized societies has been to protect the citizens and the country from aggression and oppression from external and internal forces. Currently, Americans are not safe on neighborhood streets and the incidence of violent crime in communities is everpresent. Our current penal, judicial, and correctional systems are failing to protect us and the inmates. Americans are not being well-served by these systems. Our government is failing to protect its citizens. The entire penal system of the United States needs to be overhauled.

The current correctional system is overcrowded and returns hardened, more violent, and wiser prison graduates back into our communities. Our prisons are overcrowded because of increasing crime and our change in the philosophy of how to manage crime and criminals. Crime is increasing because of the breakdown in our value systems. What has happened to family values and the work ethic?

The failure of the prison system is one symptom of a disease that is affecting our country: deterioration of our values. This is evident in the breakdown of many other major institutions such as: the banking system, the insurance-health system, the educational system, the religious institutions, the welfare system, the judicial system, and the political system. Throughout history, a common thread was woven of values such as honesty, truth, patriotism, character, justice, loyalty, and responsibility that has held the country together. That common thread that runs through the entire fabric of our societal institutions is frayed and breaking. To correct the breakdown of our institutional infrastructure, each failing system must make a "grassroots" effort to reestablish the values upon which they were founded.

The needed reform of our correctional institutions goes beyond the walls of the prison. To be effective, the reform must extend to the judicial and political arenas. The reform must extend to families, to our communities, and to our philosophies regarding crime, criminal behavior, personal safety, and domestic tranquility. The reform must touch the very values and moral standards that have held this country together for generations.

In the case of our penal institutions, we must return to the basic philosophy of why we have prisons in the first place, the *raison detre* of our correctional programs. That reason, of course, is to protect society and the citizens from the criminals and the forces of crime. Prisons were established to separate the lawbreakers that threatened society from the law-abiding citizens. They were established to punish the criminals and act as a deterrent for crime. Prisons were created as a reminder that laws must be obeyed: If they were not obeyed, there would be consequences.

Because of well-intentioned, compassionate rhetoric and the actions of a liberal activist court, we have strayed from our original demands for law and order. The rise in criminal activity and the disregard for law and order are a direct result of the liberal attitude regarding crime.

Our liberal, activist judicial system and the Supreme Court have made it evident by their rulings, that they do not want to punish crime and criminals. They have made it perfectly clear that the criminals' rights are equal to and often more equal than the rights of law-abiding citizens to be safe and secure.

Our activist judges and courts have followed a liberal political agenda that is spreading from our domestic criminal policy and is now coloring our foreign policy. Our policy makers are now advising foreign powers as to how they should conduct their internal affairs if they expect to deal with America on economic issues. Our politicians cloak these demands in the guise of "human rights" and democracy.

Sovereign nations, such as Singapore and China, who have solved their crime problems by enforcing their laws, are condemned as being harsh, cruel, and against human rights. These countries have secured peace, harmony, and safety for their law-abiding citizens. They value the rights of their citizens to live in peace more than they value the rights of the criminals.

Our politicians, with the blessing of the courts, try to stop crime control measures such as caning in Singapore, which works to deter crime, and replace them with the American "criminal rights" agenda that has proven to foster more crime. Our judicial and political emphasis is wrong. This only increases our insecurity while it emboldens the criminal and allows crime to run rampant.

We need major rethinking and reform of our correctional and judicial systems if we are going to regain our security. The task of reclaiming our peace and security is formidable. Americans have proven they do not shy away from difficult problems. Certain steps must be taken if we are to correct our present situation.

We must do the following:

1. Have a judicial system that is hard on crime. Stop plea bargaining. Insure that sentences are served; twenty years means twenty years; life means life. White-collar crime deserves equal time and punishment as does blue collar crime.

2. Change the welfare-entitlement system. Do not reward unwed mothers. Once on AFDC, no more funds will be given for future pregnancies.

3. Remove the voting rights for welfare recipients. Voting rights would be regained when they are off welfare and paying taxes.

4. Build low cost Iso-Rehab facilities that can accept all of our offenders. Protect them in an isolation unit.

5. Get the criminals off the streets. If they can not be rehabilitated; keep them behind bars.

6. Enforce our current laws; we do not need new laws.

7. Allow law-abiding citizens to arm themselves and carry concealed weapons. Felons and ex-cons would be

denied the right of a weapon.

8. Punish criminals for crimes committed. Stop treating criminals like victims of society who were forced by societal pressures to commit crime.

9. Stop programs and policies that do not rehabilitate or deter crime. Encourage programs that do work.

10. Insure that the prison experience teaches the criminal to respect law and order. A prisoner should never want to go back to prison; make the prison experience meaningful. Isolation, for an extended period, will change the criminal mentality.

11. Insure that the commission of a crime and subsequent incarceration does not qualify offenders for free education, free room and board, free medical care, and care for their family left in the community.

12. Insure that the commission of a crime earns an appropriate sentence and punishment.

A major corrective step toward these goals is the Iso-Rehab philosophy of prisoner confinement and economic prison construction. Using isolation as a tool for rehabilitation and retraining will produce better results than our present systems. The Iso-Rehab will save money and protect the prisoners, the staff, and the community. The Iso-Rehab facility and experience will give prisoners time *alone to think.*

Bibliography and References

1. Bailey, Walter C. *"Correctional Outcome: An Evaluation of 100 Reports"* Crime and Justice Vol. 3, ed. Leon Radzinowicz and Marvin E. Wolfgang. New York: Basic Books, 1971: pp. 190

2. Bender, David L. *America's Prisons - Opposing Viewpoints.* St. Paul, MN: Greenhaven Press Inc., 1980

3. Bender, David L. and McCuen, Gary E. *Crime and Criminals - Opposing Viewpoints.* St. Paul, MN: Greenhaven Press Inc., 1977

4. Copperman, Paul. *The Literacy Hoax.* New York: Morrow Quill Paperbacks, 1980

5. Department of Public Safety, Division of Criminal Justice. *Report on Crime and Justice in Colorado and Denver 1985.* Colorado: 1985

6. DiIulio, John J., Jr. *No Escape - The Future of American Corrections.* New York: Basic Books, 1991

7. Fine, Judge Ralph Adam. *Escape of the Guilty.* New York:

Dodd, Mead and Co., Inc., 1986

8. Greenberg, Reuben with Gordon, Arthur. *Let's Take Back Our Streets!* Chicago, IL: Contemporary Books, Inc., 1989

9. Hood, R. G. *"Research on the Effectiveness of Punishments and Treatments"* Crime and Justice Vol. 3, ed. Radzinowicz and Wolfgang. New York: Basic Books, 1971: pp. 159–182

10. Jarvis, Dwight C. *Institutional Treatment of the Offender.* New York: McGraw Hill, 1978

11. Lesce, Tom. *The Big House - How American Prisons Work.* Port Townsend, WA: Loompanics Unlimited, 1991

12. Long, Harold S. *Surviving in Prison.* Port Townsend, WA: Loompanics Unlimited, 1990

13. Martinson, Robert. *"What Works? - Questions and Answers about Prison Reform"* The Public Interest (Spring 1974): pp. 22–54

14. Murray, Charles. *Losing Ground.* New York: Basic Books, 1984

15. Samenow, Stanton E. *Inside the Criminal Mind.* New York: Times Books, 1984

16. Sowell, Thomas. *Ethnic America.* New York: Basic Books, 1981

17. Sowell, Thomas. *Inside American Education.* New York: Free Press, 1993

18. Taylor, Jared. *Paved With Good Intentions.* New York:

Carroll and Graf Publishers, Inc., 1992

19. U.S. Department of Justice. Office of Justice Programs. Bureau of Justice Statistics. *Correctional Populations in the United States, 1991.* Washington, D.C.: August 1993

20. U.S. Department of Justice. Office of Justice Programs. Bureau of Justice Statistics, Special Report. *The Economic Cost of Crime to Victims.* Washington D.C., April 1984

21. U.S. Department of Justice. Office of Justice Programs. Bureau of Justice Statistics, Bulletin. *Justice Expenditure and Employment, 1990.* Washington D.C., September 1992

22. U.S. Department of Justice. Office of Justice Programs. Bureau of Justice Statistics. *Justice Expenditure and Employment in the U.S., 1988.* Washington D.C., August 1991

23. U.S. Department of Justice. Office of Justice Programs. Bureau of Justice Statistics. *Prisons and Prisoners in the United States.* Washington D.C., April 1992

24. U.S. Department of Justice. Office of Justice Programs. Bureau of Justice Statistics, Special Report. *Recidivism of felons on probation, 1986-89.* Washington D.C., February 1992

25. U.S. Department of Justice. Bureau of Justice Statistics, Special Report. *Recidivism of Young Parolees.* Washington D.C., May 1987

26. U.S. Department of Justice. Office of Justice Programs. Bureau of Justice Statistics. *Survey of State Prison Inmates,*

1991. Washington D.C., March 1993

27. Wilson, James Q. *Thinking About Crime.* New York: Vintage Books, February 1985; Revised Edition

28. Yochelson, Samuel and Samenow, Stanton E. *The Criminal Personality: The Change Process, Volume 2.* New York: Jason Aronson, Inc., 1977

About the Author

As a young high school dropout, Alan joined the Marine Corps in June of 1948. After spending time on the island of Guam in the Marine barracks, he made the Inchon landing in the Korean War in September of 1950. He fought proudly with the 1st Marine Division to liberate Seoul, Korea. Following that, he fought the Communist Chinese in the Chosin Reservoir campaign in Northern Korea in November and December of 1950.

After returning to the states, Alan studied and graduated from the University of Colorado with a degree in Sociology and Psychology. He taught High School for one year, and then decided to go to Medical School. In 1961 he graduated from Medical School at the University of Tennessee.

Dr. Watts relocated to Colorado and was in General Practice of Medicine for 25 years. During that time, he helped run the Emergency Room at St. Anthony's Hospital in Denver, Colorado — one of the busiest Emergency Departments in the state.

Since his retirement, Dr. Watts is continually reminded that our crime rates are increasing and that we are no longer safe in the U.S.A. Our correctional and justice systems are broken and failing. As a doctor, Alan feels he can help the problem with the principles of Iso-Rehab as explained in "Alone to Think".